What Othe

"In my work, I see many teens who deal with some degree of social anxiety disorder. Klarner in a very personal and heartfelt way, shares her own journey with SAD and gives helpful advice on how others can overcome this disorder and go on to lead happy, fulfilled lives. Since most high school students experience some form of social anxiety and awkwardness, every teenager would benefit from reading this book!"

—Jeannette Spotts, MSSW

"*Releasing the Secret Pain* is a journey of pain and triumph over a chronic thorn in one's side – Social Anxiety Disorder. Narrative, personal account, and useful recovery strategies are interwoven throughout. Those who struggle with SAD will find it a compelling read and gain much needed identification and support."

— Gary Grahl, MSE, LPC, and author of *Skinny Boy*

"Lisa Klarner shares her own story of shyness and social anxiety. She inspires the reader through her experiences, her openness, and her faith. This memoir, written from the heart, offers gentle suggestions to all who struggle with social anxiety."

— Barbara Markway, Ph.D. and author of *Dying of Embarrassment, Painfully Shy,* and *Nurturing the Shy Child*

Releasing the Secret Pain

Moving Beyond
Social Anxiety Disorder

Releasing the Secret Pain

Moving Beyond
Social Anxiety Disorder

Lisa Klarner

Peaceful
Horizons
LLC

To my wonderful husband Greg and my amazing son Jake.

I love you both always and forever.

We want to hear from you. Please send your comments about this book to us in care of lklarner@gmail.com.

Releasing the Secret Pain
Moving Beyond Social Anxiety Disorder
Copyright © 2012 by Lisa Klarner.

P.O. Box 1914
Appleton, WI 54912
lklarner@gmail.com; http://www.releasingsocialanxiety.com

Library of Congress Control Number: 2012941408
Peaceful Horizons, LLC, Appleton, Wisconsin

ISBN-13: 978-0-9884342-0-2 (Peaceful Horizons, LLC)
ISBN-10: 0988434202

Cover Design: Cindy Gullikson
Editor: Deb DiSandro
Proofreader: Jenny Loomis
Typesetter: Deb Manning

First edition 2012

Contents

Part One – Developing the Pain

Part Two – Coping with the Pain

Part Three – Fixing the Pain

Names have been changed to protect the privacy of others.

Acknowledgements

Thank you to my husband, Greg, for your love, support and laughter as I wrote this book. Jake, my son, thanks for your smiles and hugs and for making sure I continued to have fun throughout the writing journey.

My sister, Cindy, your creativity and patience in the design process made the steps seem so much easier. Mom and Dad, thanks for teaching me to be a hard-working, determined adult. Without these traits, I never would have finished this book. My sister, Shelley, and my brother, Jeremy, thanks for your support and love along the way.

Pam, Tanya and Wendy, thanks for being such great friends and for reminiscing about the past with me as I wrote this book. Thank you to all the friends and co-workers who listened to me talk about my book over the years. Your kindness and support was appreciated.

This book never would have come to fruition if it weren't for my writing coach and editor, Deb. Your encouragement in the tedious writing process was just what I needed. Thanks for helping me grow as a writer.

My proofreader, Jenny, your attention to detail was exactly what I needed. You helped me to focus more on the content and less on the grammar.

Thank you to the writing friends I met along the way at the Green Lake Christian Writers Conference and the University of Minnesota Writers Workshop. Your encouragement helped me to continue moving forward.

Most importantly, thank you God for answering my prayers by allowing me to feel true peace in my life and for guiding the right people into my life at the right time.

Intended Audience

❖ Teens who let shyness or social anxiety stop them from making friends, contributing to classroom discussions and dating

❖ Parents of children with social anxiety disorder

❖ Teachers, counselors or social workers

❖ Anyone who struggles with social anxiety, has difficulty meeting new people, making new friends and valuing and voicing their own opinions

How to Use This Book

For anyone dealing with shyness, social anxiety disorder (SAD) or general social fears:

This book is a guide to help you better understand your feelings and coping mechanisms. Whether you are a teen or an adult, you will read about techniques that you can use to ease your mind, increase your confidence and live a life without fear. I will share stories from my own life to help you understand what may be happening to you. As you work through the book, give yourself time to take the information in, process it, and begin to understand your own experiences. Answer the questions I have included within the chapters to reflect on what you are learning, and make note of any other questions or experiences that come to mind as you read.

For anyone who has a child or student struggling with shyness or social anxiety disorder:

This book will help you to better understand the individual challenged by SAD. Most of the battles associated with SAD play out in a person's own mind; therefore, it may be difficult to determine – from outside appearances –what's really happening. Throughout the book, I will be talking directly to the person who is dealing with shyness or SAD. This book will also give you some tools and techniques to help the person you care for begin to heal. You may even find value in using some of the resources for your own benefit.

Disclaimer

The views and information expressed in this publication are those of the author and are not meant to dictate, guide, or provide medical treatment. The information presented in this book is for advisory purposes only. The information given is neither medical advice nor is it presented as a course of personalized treatment. Use of the information in this publication does not replace proper medical care provided by your qualified health or medical practitioner. Any application of the material set forth in the following pages is at the reader's discretion and is the reader's sole responsibility. The author disclaims responsibility for the application of the information contained herein.

Every attempt has been made to assure that the information presented in this book is correct, but there remains the possibility of error, for which the author cannot be held responsible.

The Food and Drug Administration (FDA) has not evaluated any of the statements or contents of this publication. The information contained herein is NOT intended, nor should it be used, to diagnose, treat, cure, prevent, or mitigate any disease or condition.

THE AUTHOR AND THE PUBLISHER DISCLAIM ANY LIABILITY ARISING DIRECTLY OR INDIRECTLY FROM THE USE OF THIS BOOK.

Foreword

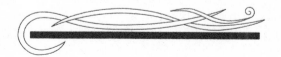

About 15% of people are born with a tendency to be more shy and withdrawn compared to others. A portion of these individuals will develop anxiety disorders that make it difficult for them to do things like go to school or work, get along with peers, and get their work done. Social anxiety disorder tends to develop in late childhood or early adolescence and often lasts for many years, especially if it goes untreated. Large-scale studies suggest that it affects 5-12% of individuals at some point in their lives. Yet, most people do not receive treatment, and thus suffer in silence. In this book, Lisa Klarner offers hope for those experiencing social anxiety. She expertly weaves her own story into an interactive guide for youth who may be experiencing similar emotions.

In adolescence, close peer relationships are an important source of social support. Self-consciousness about social situations is a normal part of development during adolescence. However, children with social anxiety find navigating peer relationships to be particularly challenging. They may feel embarrassed speaking up in class, initiating a conversation with a peer, or eating in front of others in the cafeteria. In severe cases, a child may refuse to go to school.

Although social anxiety disorder is quite distressing for the child experiencing it, it may go undetected by friends, teachers, or even parents. Often times children with social anxiety experience upsetting thoughts like *No one likes me, I'm not as good at things as other kids,* or *If I say the wrong thing, others will make fun of me.* Regardless of the validity of these thoughts, children with social anxiety believe they are true and subsequently feel anxious. Children with social anxiety may spend a lot of time thinking about past interpersonal experiences that did not go well along with worrying about whether they will be rejected in the future. Most of us do not realize that getting caught up in our thoughts like this can make us more anxious. One of the most effective treatments for social anxiety involves helping people realize the connection between thoughts and feelings.

If you are a young person with anxiety about social situations or if you are the loved one of a child with social anxiety disorder, you will likely find this book extremely helpful. In this book, Lisa Klarner does several things that may help a young person with social anxiety. First of all, she normalizes the experience of anxiety by sharing her own personal accounts of anxiety throughout her life. She conveys a message of acceptance, which seems to be an important element in recovering from an anxiety disorder. None of us like to experience negative emotions like anxiety, but rather than fighting against the anxiety, accepting the emotion and being able to let it go is helpful in long run.

Another really important aspect of this book is that Klarner helps the reader make connections between thoughts and feelings. She includes short exercises at the end of each chapter that help facilitate these connections and makes reading this book engaging and interactive. Klarner also recommends social interaction throughout the book. She uses positive encouragement to help anxious youth engage with their peers. Research has shown that exposure to feared situations is one of the most important aspects of overcoming anxiety. Thus, if this book can inspire you to engage with other youth, you will be well on your way to releasing the secret pain and moving beyond social anxiety disorder.

Lori M. Hilt, Ph.D.
Assistant Professor
Lawrence University
Department of Psychology

Introduction

Do you struggle with extreme shyness? Does it feel like people are always watching you? Do you wonder why you seem to attract bullies? Do you wish you could understand this painful self-consciousness and find a way to stop the inner turmoil that plagues you every day?

I understand how you feel. These are feelings I struggled with for nearly 20 years before I finally discovered that my shyness had become a disorder called social anxiety disorder. The Social Anxiety Institute defines social anxiety as follows:

❖ Social anxiety is the fear of social situations and the interaction with other people that can automatically bring on feelings of self-consciousness, judgment, evaluation, and inferiority.

❖ Put another way, social anxiety is the fear and anxiety of being judged and evaluated negatively by other people, leading to feelings of inadequacy, embarrassment, humiliation, and depression.

❖ If a person usually becomes anxious in social situations, but seems fine when they are alone, then "social anxiety" may be the problem.

❖ Social anxiety disorder (formerly termed "social phobia") is a much more common problem than past estimates have led us to believe. Millions of people all over the world suffer from this devastating and traumatic problem every day, either from a specific social anxiety or from a more generalized social anxiety.

❖ In the United States, epidemiological studies have recently pegged social anxiety disorder as the third largest psychological disorder in the country, after depression and alcoholism. It is estimated that 7-8% of the population suffers from some form of social anxiety at the present time. The lifetime prevalence rate for developing social anxiety disorder is 13-14%. *(Richards)*

Check out the Understanding SAD
section of my website for more
information on understanding SAD:
www.releasingsocialanxiety.com/understanding

I am not a doctor or a medical expert; I'm a person who has suffered from SAD, and I want to help you. As I wrote this book, I wondered how different my life would be if I could start over from the beginning. Would I really want my past to be different? What if I never suffered from The Secret Pain of social anxiety disorder? Would I be the same person I am today if the painful events of my past had never happened? Of that, I'm not sure, but what I am sure of is this: I'm done living in fear. When the old, familiar feelings crop back up and fear takes control of my body… heart races… palms sweat… breathing constricts… I remind myself that

I'm done with this fear and center myself with these comforting words:

Calm down.

Breathe.

People respect me.

They are kind.

Others are focused on themselves; they don't pay as much attention to me as I think they do.

My faith in God has been a large part of my journey and you will read about my doubts and hopes when it comes to God's involvement in my life. You may not believe in God; you may just believe in a "higher power." It is my hope for you that you have faith in "someone" or "something" to help you through difficult times and to give you the support you may need. When I reference God, just interchange His name with that of your higher power.

If you are extremely shy or if you believe you have SAD, you may be too afraid to talk to anyone about it. You accept that life is painful for you – you tell yourself, *This is just the way it is going to be.* In this day and age, it's very easy to be removed from society with the Internet, chat rooms and texting. For a good part of the day, you can get by without really connecting face-to-face with anyone, but what type of life is that? Life can be full of joy for you. It doesn't need to be full of fear and loneliness – THERE IS HOPE! My goal is to help you become more confident and begin to overcome SAD. Reading this book is a big step in your healing journey, and I'm very excited to be a part of your experience.

Part One

Developing the Pain

Chapter One

When Does Shyness Start?

"By His light I walked through darkness."
- Job 29:3, New International Version

I wasn't born shy. According to my mom, I was quite the popular kid at age three. When she pushed me all over town in the stroller, I would smile and wave, happily greeting everyone we met. The year I turned five, everything changed. Something terrible happened: I began school. But that was only the half of it. I was also expected to ride on the big, bulging, belching, yellow thing called "the bus."

September 1974
Five years old, Kindergarten

The school bus roared toward my house, a tiger ready to pounce upon its tiny, trembling prey. The security of Mom's presence would soon be gone. It was my first bus ride on the first day of kindergarten, and according to my mom's memory and my own distant recall, I was terrified...

"No, don't make me go on the bus!" I cried. "I'm so scared, Mommy!" I wrapped my arms around Mom's legs, looking up at her with terror in my eyes, praying she would save me from the fast-approaching tiger.

She didn't save me but tried to instill comfort.

"I'm sorry, Lisa. I know you are scared," she said as she bent down and hugged me. I tried to stop the tears, my chest heaving in and out.

"But we don't have a choice; you need to go on the bus. It will be okay," Mom assured me while the big, scary, yellow thing crept closer.

The tiger stopped inches from my new patent leather shoes and opened its mouth wide, ready to gobble me up.

Mom pried my sweaty hands off of her.

My heart raced. I tried to stop the tears so the kids on the bus wouldn't see me crying.

Only partially successful, I glanced up through tear-stained eyes, just high enough to see the huge steps looming before me. I contemplated turning around and running into the safety of Mom's arms and my cozy home, but the distance between Mom and me was growing too quickly. I hesitantly climbed the steps and slid into the first seat, my body visibly trembling. I avoided eye contact. Voices of excited children hovered like a cloud over my fearful mind.

Was it normal for me, at age five, to be afraid of my first bus ride? Sure, most kids probably are; it's just that people show their fear in different ways. Some kids who are naturally outgoing can get over their fears more easily, while others who are naturally shy find it difficult to deal with new situations. Everyone is unique, with God-given qualities. The traits that a child may consider "bad," such as shyness, are often traits that God wants him to have for some purpose – a life lesson. Besides, if we were all the same, the world would be a boring place.

I wonder how Mom must have felt when she had to pry my sweaty hands off of her and send me, trembling with fear, onto the bus. Any insecurities and fear she was keeping at bay may have validated my own insecurities.

I remember Mom being outgoing and social when I was a child, but I found out in recent years that she had the same types of fears that I've experienced in my life. She told me she doesn't like people looking at her and that she was extremely shy growing up. It is possible Mom may have masked her insecurities in hopes that her children wouldn't experience the same types of fears. Or maybe it was simply that Mom learned how to cope with her anxiety to survive. Did I inherit my shyness? Did I learn this behavior from Mom even though I don't remember her being shy or anxious? Or would my challenges with shyness have happened no matter what type of parent I ended up with in this life?

According to child and family therapist, Dr. Andrea "Andie" Weiner, there are several reasons why children become shy:

> Sometimes children are born with a temperament that creates them to be more sensitive and reactive to new situations... There are some studies that also show that shyness runs in families. How much is hereditary and how much is learned and modeled behavior is not quite discernible... A third reason is the child's lack of experience in social situations... if they have not learned how to effectively be part of social situations, they may become frightened and withdraw. Another cause of shyness is low self-esteem which causes the child to have low opinions of themselves ... Lastly, children that are overprotected do not have the chance to become socially independent. Because of this overprotection, they don't have the opportunity to develop confidence to make decisions for themselves. This creates that cycle of insecurity which leads to shyness *(Weiner)*.

> For more advice from Dr. Andrea "Andie" Weiner, check out her books, *More Than Saying I Love You* and *The Best Investment: Understanding The Secrets of Social Success for Your Child,* and her website, www.drandie.com.

You may have your own ideas as to where your shyness came from. Maybe you were the victim of physical or verbal abuse at some point in your life, which contributed to low self-esteem. Perhaps you had a specific situation or medical problem that caused your insecurities to develop.

A friend of mine, Mary, always remembers being shy and this shyness may have begun long before school started. At age 3, Mary had a heart murmur and had to spend a few days in the hospital away from her mother. She remembers being extremely afraid. And from that one event, the shyness and anxiety grew. In school, Mary worried about being called on in class. She wouldn't participate in extracurricular activities because of her crippling fear. Her mom didn't force her to join sports, even though she knew Mary had athletic ability, because she felt it would have worsened the debilitating shyness. Being in the spotlight was, and still is, an anxiety-producing experience for Mary. On the other hand, her older sister was confident, outgoing, and enthusiastic about joining extra-curricular activities. She was very social. Was Mary's shyness a part of her genetic make-up? What caused her personality to be so different from that of her sister?

Whatever the reason for Mary's introversion, she survived her shyness and is a successful mom and social worker today.

When Mary had a son, she noticed he had a shy disposition right from the start. He was afraid of other kids and adults. Mary often worried about her son's personality development and didn't want him to experience the struggles with shyness that she experienced growing up. At home, he would be outgoing and confident, but in social situations, he had a hard time. He would attach himself to her. Her son was introverted and had a hard time asserting himself throughout his childhood. Rather than being confident and speaking out about concerns, he repressed his anger and avoided or quit activities like sports. Mary pushed him to do things he may not have wanted to do, hoping he could get past the paralyzing fear he experienced whenever he anticipated being in the spotlight. Maybe pushing her son to interact with other kids helped him to overcome his shyness, or maybe he would have grown more confident on his own. Regardless, Mary's son is an assertive and social adult today.

The reason for a person's shyness doesn't matter much; what matters is what that person decides to do about it. A person can accept it or decide to change it gently. But those of us, including me, who saw shyness as a "bad" quality tried to ignore it which caused it to grow. Life experiences, coupled with my own doubts, fears, and negative thought patterns, further justified my perceptions that shyness was bad.

It might be helpful for you to look at the past to understand why you may be shy, but don't dwell on it. Explore it gently, and then move on. Focus on the present and allow yourself to heal.

Take Action!

Be an observer today. See how others around you are interacting with each other.

List the reason(s) why you think you might be shy:

_____

_____

_____

Think of people you know who are shy. What qualities do you like about those people?

_____

_____

_____

List three positives in your life, such as someone or something that makes you smile and feel at ease:

1. _____

_____

2. _____

_____

3. _____

_____

Chapter Two

Dealing with Bullies

"I've learned that people will forget what you said, people will forget what you did, but people will never forget how you made them feel."
- Maya Angelou

As soon as I started school, the bullying began. Bullies were drawn to me because I was timid and visibly insecure. When I was at school, on the playground, or on the bus, the bullies would knock books out of my hands, call me names, or pull my hair. It must have been very satisfying for the bullies to see my reaction to their assaults: tears, blushing, trembling. My parents knew something was happening because I would run off the bus, storm into the house, slam the bedroom door, and collapse on my bed in a fit of tears. I was too afraid to talk about it. When my parents asked what was happening, I would say "nothing," or when they asked what was wrong, I would say, "I don't know." The bullying was difficult enough for me, and then my younger sister, Victoria, started school. Now I had double the trouble ...

August 1980
Eleven years old, 6th grade

We stepped out of the comfort of our home; the dew on the green grass glistened as the rays of sun peeked through the clouds. *Maybe this year will be different,* I thought. *Maybe they will ignore me or be nice. Please, God, make it different,* I prayed as I walked with my five-year-old sister, Victoria, to the end of our driveway. Victoria was starting kindergarten. Her long brown hair was combed to perfection and her big brown eyes shone wide with innocence. We stood hand in hand at the end of the driveway waiting for the bus.

My legs trembled and my hands were slick with sweat as the bus sputtered to a stop. Victoria was frightened and she needed me – her big sister – to comfort her, but my own mounting fear overpowered any protective instincts I may have had for my little sister. I was so afraid that, surely, my fear must have transferred to her, the sweat on my own palms dampening her tiny hands.

The tiger looked bigger this year. What if there were even more bullies? Would I survive the attacks? Victoria and I slid into a seat toward the front of the bus, as the voices of the bullies, Tom and Martin, began to taunt me.

"Well, lookie here! It's four eyes and her little sister." Tom's mouth formed into a devilish smile.

Wham! A spitball hit me.

"Score!" Martin gave Tom a high five to congratulate him on the successful shot.

Laughter echoed through the bus and I felt sure it was directed at me.

My hands shook and my eyes filled with tears. Heat turned my neck and face from a golden tan to a sunburned red. The trapped feeling I experienced the year before returned as a grim reminder of my reality.

There was no way out.

Through the tears, I managed to look at my sister. "Victoria, just ignore them. It will be okay. Not too much longer now."

Tom and Martin slithered around the bus, continuing to torment other kids, and periodically coming back to me, all the way to school.

That night at dinner, the aroma of pot roast filled the dining room. Silverware scraped against plates, ice cubes clinked in glasses, and the antics of those shipwrecked on *Gilligan's Island* blared from the television occasionally interrupting family conversation.

Victoria's tiny voice broke through the idle chatter. "On the bus today a boy was calling Lisa names, and another boy spit a paper ball at her head. Why are those boys so mean, Mommy?" Victoria looked longingly at Mom for an answer. In a five-year-old's world, life was simple. She couldn't comprehend why kids would be so mean.

I absently moved food around my plate with my fork, hoping Victoria's comment would be discounted as nothing more than the workings of a child's wild imagination.

Mom frowned and looked over at me. "Lisa, what's going on? I know you are upset when you get home from school, but you won't talk to me."

I looked up at Mom and saw the love and concern in her eyes. How badly I wanted to tell her of the torment!

Memories of bullies pulling my hair and shoving me flashed through my mind, but the words wouldn't come out. I pushed my chair back, ran to my room, and slammed the door. I flopped onto my bed as the tears poured out and sadness enveloped my heart.

Mom came into my room and sat down on the bed beside me, rubbing her hand gently across my back. "Lisa, honey, how long has this been going on?"

In between breathless sobs, I blurted out, "Quite a while."

"Who is doing this to you?"

"Tom and… and… Martin." I gasped for air. "They… they… are… on… my bus and Tom is in my class."

Mom hugged me and her warmth and love momentarily melted away my fears. "We will take care of this for you, sweetie," she assured me. "Your dad and I will make it all better."

Once my parents found out about the bullying, thanks to Victoria, my dad called the bus company and gave them a piece of his mind. The bullying stopped for a while, but in time, the attacks started up again. I was too ashamed to tell my parents that I couldn't fend for myself. It was embarrassing to be so weak and afraid. On top of that, once the bullies started up again, they added snide remarks about 'crying to mommy.' It was hopeless. The bullying would never end. The teachers and bus driver turned a blind eye to the attacks because, in their eyes, it was just harmless teasing.

In discussing bullies with Mom and Dad recently, I found out that they were also bullied as children. Mom said she never told me this when I was young because it didn't seem like the right approach. She worried that I would feel as though she were minimizing my issues, making me feel like I should just 'get over it.' I don't know how I would have reacted at age eleven if she had told me that she, too, had been bullied, but it's likely I wouldn't have believed her because in my mind, no one understood how terrible my situation was.

My parents' life challenges taught them the value of having empathy for others and a strong work ethic, and today they are successful business owners. Sure, Mom still remembers how as a child she envied the way other kids were dressed while the bullies teased her about the old, worn-out clothes she had to wear. Mom also remembers another girl from school who was bullied because she was a "farm girl." She was insecure socially, and the bullies latched on to her and teased her often. Did the bully attacks cause her to live a less-than-successful life? No. As a matter of fact, this farm girl ended up having ten kids and is a multi-millionaire today!

Kids who are bullied, or who have a hard life in general, can take their pain and sadness and divert that energy toward living a life full of happiness, or they can repress their anger about the past and fall into a deep depression. Even though it may be difficult for you to see now, it is my hope that you will eventually choose happiness. You will be able to use the good and bad experiences from your past to help you grow.

At age eleven, I knew, as I said earlier, that I couldn't say anything to my parents about the attacks starting up again. They would have taken action if I told them what was happening, so I started internalizing my emotional distress when I was at home. How did I do it? Was it denial? Acceptance? I found that pretending to be indifferent worked best. Rather than storming into the house and slamming my bedroom door, I would walk in with little emotion. When Mom would ask me how my day was, I would just say, "Okay." I would force my lips to curve up into a smile, while inside I was sad and angry about the bullies' attacks of the day. Internalizing my feelings became a common practice; I became rather good at it, but at what cost? Mom thought the bullies were leaving me alone, but one day she witnessed them firsthand...

October 1980
Eleven years old, 6th grade

Leaning against the wall with Victoria, I peered up occasionally, hoping for Mom's quick arrival. She was picking us up from school because I had a doctor appointment. Kids stood nearby waiting for the bus, including Tom. I fidgeted nervously with the books that didn't fit into my bulging backpack, hoping to avoid unwelcome attention. Finally, Mom pulled up in our big, blue Lincoln Continental.   '

Tom saw an opportunity to tease me and he took it. "Look! Richy's mom is here to pick her up! Richy! Richy!" he chanted.

Quickly, I jumped into the car after Victoria and threw my backpack on the floor.

Splat! A gob of spit hit the back window.

I looked out the window and saw Tom giving Martin a high five and laughing.

Mom was shocked when the spit hit the window. She gave me a questioning look but didn't press for more information. I shrugged it off as if nothing had happened, but inside I felt sick, disgusted, and fearful all at the same time.

Maybe you have had similar – or worse – experiences with bullying. My heart goes out to you. It's hard to believe the old adage *Sticks and stones will break my bones, but words will never hurt me.* I know you probably want me to say it's true, that words won't hurt you, but I can't. Words do hurt! Physical attacks are even worse and can vary greatly in severity. In both cases, the emotional turmoil can wreak havoc on the victim.

Years later, I've learned a few things about bullying. First, I know it's extremely important for those of you who are being bullied to tell someone. If the first person you tell makes you feel like the accusations are all in your head, find someone else because that person isn't the right person to help you. Friends may be empathetic and try to protect you, but they usually don't understand how you feel and can't stop the bullying from happening. Talk to a parent, teacher, guidance counselor, or trusted adult. Someone will believe you. Someone will help you. It will get better.

Bullies are full of fear themselves.

The second thing I've learned about bullying is that the bullies are often full of fear themselves. Rather than turning their fear inward and appearing shy (as you and I do), they act out and hurt others. Bullies commonly have abusive home lives and take their anger out on the kids who appear weak – the easy targets. I don't necessarily want you to feel sorry for the bullies, but I want you to understand why they may be acting the way they do.

Take Action!

Look around. See if other kids are being bullied. Observe the bully. Is he really just afraid? How does he act when he isn't lashing out at someone?

Today, I wonder what type of life Tom had. Did he have a loving home like mine, or was his family life full of anger, conflict and neglect? Recently, I was talking to one of my best friends from high school about my experiences with being bullied. When I reminded her who the bully was, she was surprised because she said that Tom (who still lives in the town I grew up in) is a great parent to his children, is well liked by many and is genuinely nice.

When I finished sixth grade in the Catholic grade school, I moved to the public school for seventh grade. By this point, bullying was a common occurrence in my everyday school life, whether it be a passing rude comment or a spitball landing in my hair. I felt The Secret Pain growing inside me. A few symptoms were becoming more problematic. Blushing was the main concern, followed by trembling and sweating. When Tom would attack, sweat would run down my back and my face and neck would turn red. A visible reaction meant success for Tom! He kept on coming back for more. The symptoms I experienced during bully attacks started happening more frequently in other scenarios, such as sitting in class, speaking up in class, or walking down the hallway. The Secret Pain took root and reared its ugly head more often now.

Although I didn't recognize it at the time, I wasn't alone. There was a boy on my bus named Randy. He was extremely shy like me. The bullies attacked him too, but I was too closed off by my own fear to really notice. A couple of years later, Randy hanged himself in his parents' basement at age thirteen. I'll never know if the incessant bullying caused him to commit suicide, but I believe it contributed to his problems. If only I had noticed he was so afraid, maybe we could have banded together to support each other. Maybe I could have helped him to see that suicide wasn't the answer. After he died, kids were friendlier and kinder than before. Everyone seemed like they cared so much about Randy, yet when he was alive, they teased or ignored him. It was only a matter of time before the old behaviors returned – the bullying, the cliques, and the judgmental glances.

October 1981
Twelve years old, 7th grade

Long hallways.

Unfamiliar faces.

Teachers expecting more class participation.

Everything was headed in the wrong direction for a person with SAD.

Brushing pieces of eraser off my desk, I refocused on doodling in my notebook, the monotone voice of my social studies teacher barely reaching my consciousness.

"Lisa, what is your opinion?"

Jolted out of my daze, I could feel my face heat up as quickly as the flame on a match. When I realized I had no idea what the teacher was talking about, my embarrassment grew. Flicking my pencil around, I attempted to find words in my notebook that might apply. Nothing. "Um... oh... I'm not sure...."

The teacher moved on to other students while my thoughts swirled down a black hole. *Stupid idiot! How embarrassing! You never do anything right!*

The bell rang. Unsure if I would rather be sitting in misery in the classroom or walking into the jungle of students in the hallway, I reluctantly slid out of my desk.

Voices of students moving from one class to another echoed through the halls. The walls felt like they were closing in on me. My shoulders sank as the social studies incident slithered through my mind.

A short while later, I was sitting in homeroom next to my new best friend, Rachel. A chill ran through me when I saw Tom, the bully, swaggering over.

Tom snatched my new pencil case, his voice piercing me like a knife. "Look at what Lisa has! It's a fart bag!" he sneered.

Tom put my pencil case by his butt and ripped the Velcro open over and over.

Rachel jumped up and came face to face with Tom. "Give that back to her!" Rachel grabbed the pencil case and gave it back to me.

I cowered in embarrassment.

Tom hovered around us, his evil laugh penetrating my skin.

Rachel didn't back down. "Leave us alone or I will tell the teacher."

Tom shrugged his shoulders, indicating he couldn't care less if Rachel told the teacher, but he walked away anyway.

Covering my forehead with my trembling hand, I glanced over at Rachel with damp eyes. "Tom is such a jerk." "Yeah. Maybe one of these days he will grow up!"

Rachel reached out to me in friendship when we met on the first day of seventh grade. She was friendly and outgoing. I found comfort and security in her presence. She sat next to me in homeroom and protected me as much as she could. If it wasn't for friends like Rachel, school would have been much worse. My wish for you is that you find a friend or two who will stick by you and stick up for you, someone you can lean on in times of trouble.

If you are bullied, I empathize with you and know that it is difficult to let go of the incident. You may even re-live the situation over and over in your mind like I did. According to PACER's National Bullying Prevention Center website, more than 160,000 U.S. students stay home from school each day from fear of being bullied (PACER Center). Some kids laugh off the attacks, almost instantly forgetting about them. Others remember the confrontations, but do not let the memories influence their lives in a negative way. Still others dwell on the incidents, reliving them many times in their minds and feeling like they are the only ones who have had these horrible experiences. I am a dweller. We dwellers internalize our anger because of our own inability to stick up for ourselves and stop the attacks. The fearful memories creep into all the crevices in our minds.

There must be a good number of dwellers in our society because the number of bully awareness campaigns is growing, from commercials on television to speakers at schools to websites devoted solely to bully awareness.

Typically the organizers behind bully awareness campaigns are people who were attacked by bullies themselves or who have children who were attacked.

Compared to when I was a kid, bullying may be even more prevalent today. One reason is that kids may simply be looking for more attention, which they inadvertently receive when they misbehave and lash out at the weak kids at school. The second reason is technology, specifically social networks and texting. It doesn't take much courage to bully someone by posting a nasty comment on his or her facebook page or by sending a verbally abusive text message.

Take Action!

If someone is bullying you on a social network or via text messages, remove that person as a friend and block their number on your cell phone. Take control because you deserve kindness and respect.

Bullies will always exist. It is my hope that the number of bullies will decline, resulting in fewer victims. Perhaps the bully awareness campaigns will make a difference, as researchers find out more about the cause and impact of bullying. Recent messages are asking bystanders to intervene and drawing more attention to the bullies and the behavioral therapy they may need. According to PACER's National Bullying Prevention Center website, bullying directly affects a student's ability to learn. Students who are bullied find it difficult to concentrate, show a decline in grades, and lose self-esteem, self-confidence, and self-worth (PACER Center).

❖ Students who are bullied report more physical symptoms, such as headaches or stomachaches, and mental health issues, such as depression and anxiety, than other students.

❖ In some cases, bullying has led to devastating consequences, such as school shootings and suicide.

❖ Bullying affects witnesses as well as targets. Witnesses often report feeling unsafe, helpless, and afraid that they will be the next target.

❖ Bullying is a communitywide issue that must no longer be ignored or thought of as a rite of passage. Students, parents, and educators all have a role in addressing bullying situations and changing school culture.

❖ The two keys to creating change are: increasing awareness that bullying has lifelong impact, and giving people the tools they need to respond effectively.

❖ Students can be especially effective in bullying intervention. More than 55 percent of bullying situations will stop when a peer intervenes. Student education of how to address bullying for peers is critical, as is the support of adults.

❖ Silence is no longer an acceptable response to bullying. Adults, students, and educators can no longer look away when they see bullying. Ignoring it won't work. Everyone needs to be empowered with options to respond.
(PACER Center)

For more information on bullying,
check out my website
www.releasingsocialanxiety.com/bullies

I thought of Randy when I read about "bullycide: a term used to describe suicide as the result of bullying" *(Bullying Statistics 2010)*. It is disheartening to know that bullying is still negatively impacting so many lives that there is a term for suicide associated with this type of abuse. Bullycide is the biggest cost of hiding, ignoring, and internalizing these incidences, and that is why I encourage you to confide in someone you trust. Tell a friend. Let your parents know what is happening. Taking your own life may seem like the only solution. IT'S NOT! I never contemplated suicide no matter how miserable I felt. You need to look around you and see something – even a really small thing – that is good in your life. Maybe you have a great relationship with a sister or brother. Maybe you have a best friend. Maybe the fact that you are healthy and alive today is what is good about your life. I understand this time of your life is unbearably hard. It will pass. You will get through it. Your future can and will be different. Your present can be different too if you open up to someone now.

The major difference about bullying today, compared to when I was growing up, is that in most instances the bully will be held accountable for his or her actions. Remember, it's all about what you do after the experience is over. If it's a minor name-calling incident, try to let it go rather than dwelling on it. Focus on the positive aspects of your day. This will take time, but I know that you will be able to do this as you begin to move forward in your healing journey.

What is it that is causing your emotional pain?

_____

_____

_____

If you are bullied or are dealing with an emotionally draining situation, list the name of a person you will seek help from:

_____

Do you have a friend, family member or classmate who is struggling with bullying? What can you can do to help that person?

_____

_____

_____

_____

_____

Chapter Three

The Turning Point: Shyness Becomes SAD

"Don't be afraid of the dark. Remember, we need the night to see the stars."
- Joey Reiman

School life progressed. My fellow classmates and I settled into a routine. As eighth graders, we began to discover our own interests and took advantage of the many extracurricular activities that were offered. Some students joined sports from football to cross-country, while others joined band or choir and yet others participated in chess club or library club.

I loved music and singing so I joined choir. Yes, the terribly shy one joined choir! How is that possible, you may wonder? I discovered that music replaced my fears with joy, calmed my mind and allowed peace to flow through me. Choir was the one time when I actually let go of negative thoughts and really, truly enjoyed school. Unfortunately, that peace was shattered when the choir teacher gave out assignments for the winter competition. When Mrs. Sanford announced that I would be performing a solo, fear wrapped around me like a shirt that was two sizes too small. *Was she crazy? Me? Sing a solo in front of an audience?* In spite of the fear, my love of singing was stronger and kept me moving forward. I practiced and accepted the fact that I was going to sing a solo.

Leading up to the big event, I prayed to God for support and confidence. I practiced in front of my parents, in choir class, and by myself. Being prepared eased my mind a little. I learned that preparation often lessened my anxiety about presenting or performing in front of others, but the day I sat outside the room waiting for my turn to perform, I found it difficult to breathe...

December 1982
Thirteen years old, 8th grade

Sitting outside the judges' room, waiting to perform, I wrung my shaking, sweat-drenched hands together and closed my eyes in an attempt to bring a moment of peace to my mind. I tried to breathe like Mrs. Sanford taught me: in, out, deep into my stomach. No luck. *I'm going to screw up.*

I'm not going to remember the words. Everyone will be looking at me. I will be the center of attention...
Mrs. Sanford walked over. "Lisa, are you okay?"
I glanced up at Mrs. Sanford with fear-filled eyes. Unable to respond, I listened as she continued: "You are going to do great today! I have all the confidence in the world that you will sing beautifully, as always."
Mrs. Sanford's deep brown eyes showed kindness, and her smile reflected support.
I managed to say, "Thanks," and muttered something about being okay.
Mrs. Sanford reached over and gently squeezed my shoulder. "Great, because it's time for your performance."
Mrs. Sanford and I entered the room. My eyes locked on the floor, my heart raced, and beads of sweat broke out around my blushing face.
Standing in front of the small audience (although it didn't look small that day), I peered up and looked around the room. Judgmental eyes awaited my performance. Negative thoughts cropped up like stubborn weeds in a garden. *I CAN'T DO THIS! What am I doing up here? This is CRAZY! They are already laughing at me. I will be the laughing stock of the entire competition...*
One of the judges stopped my thoughts when he said, "Okay, Lisa. Start any time."
Mrs. Sanford began playing the piano, and I focused on remembering the words. I started out slow and shaky, but as I continued singing, I felt like a different person. When I sang, I often felt like I was outside of my body, which is also what happened when I gave speeches at school.
For just a moment, as I lost myself in the song, I was no longer the shy, terrified girl named Lisa, but once I sang the last note, I felt like collapsing. The anticipation of the event, the fear taunting me during the performance – it was exhausting.

I noticed that the judges were smiling at me and one said, "Great job, Lisa!"

I glanced up shyly, "Thank you."

Mrs. Sanford and I left the room. "Lisa, you did great. I knew you would!"

Mrs. Sanford walked away and my thoughts took over. *A great job! Yeah – right! My voice was shaking. I tripped over words. I looked like a nervous wreck. How humiliating! I'm sure everyone could see how embarrassed I was. I knew I would screw up something. I'm surprised they even let me finish.*

Shockingly, I received first place for my solo. Of course, I didn't feel I deserved it. Nevertheless, Mrs. Sanford continued to challenge me. She knew I was shy, but she kept pushing me out of my comfort zone. Unfortunately, at this point, my self-esteem was too far gone and I didn't know how to change the downward spiral that was increasing in speed. While I truly loved singing and the sense of peace it gave me, the fear won the battle and by ninth grade, I dropped out of choir.

Allowing your fears to win allows them to grow.

There may be times when you really want to do something, like join a club, and you feel joy and warmth in your heart. Then, the negative thoughts may take over; the warmth in your heart turns into a knot in your stomach. Your mind won't let you experience this excitement. Your fears always win. Allowing your fears to win allows them to grow. It took me years to understand that being courageous in the midst of fear would gradually build my confidence. Eventually, courage will squash fear, and when you experience that sense of accomplishment, it will warm your heart and give you even more courage and confidence. Don't wait for years to experience this, like I did. Once you have gradually started healing from SAD, you will feel the courage squashing the fear. It is possible!

Take Action!

Scan through the clubs and extra-curricular activities at your school. Set a goal for something you want to join in the future.

What do you love to do that calms your mind?

_____

_____

As you heal from SAD, what are two steps you will take to incorporate activities you love into your life?

1._____

2._____

List a situation or two where you felt you were visibly full of fear, but others commented on how well you did. Can you see now that maybe your fear wasn't that obvious after all?

_____

_____

_____

_____

As I started ninth grade, the pressure to fit in, the cliques, and my fear of being judged haunted me every minute of every day. I became an expert at hiding The Secret Pain from my friends and family. There was only one time when I talked to a friend about my deepest fear: blushing. I would talk often on the phone with my friend Lila, whom I knew from grade school. After one of Tom's bully attacks, I called her and said, "If only I could put a quarter in a jar for every time I blushed, then maybe it wouldn't happen so much." I waited with bated breath for Lila's response.

"It's not a big deal," Lila said. "A lot of people get embarrassed." She told me that I shouldn't worry about it.

Before that night, I had never said the "blushing" word to anyone. The Secret Pain – and my unknown, unexplainable fear of embarrassment – was an inherent part of me now.

I was actually sorry I told Lila. Even though she was a close friend, I feared she would begin to look at me, purely out of curiosity, to see my reactions when I blushed. What good did it do to communicate my pain if I would become even more concerned about what people thought of me – even my best friend? Even though I knew Lila thought the best of everyone, especially her friends, telling her made me realize I could never tell anyone about The Secret Pain ever again.

You may be afraid to open up about your struggles, as I was. Perhaps you weren't even aware of what was wrong until you started reading this book. Understanding the reasons for the pain you are experiencing is step one, and then, you can begin to share. I discovered that opening up is the key to healing. Take small steps as you begin to share and communicate your struggles. Small steps really do add up!

September 1984
Fifteen years old, 9th grade

Certain aspects of school were more challenging for me than others. It was easier to hide The Secret Pain in English class (unless I had to give a speech) than it was in gym. Gym class was miserable. I thought things couldn't get any worse, but in ninth grade they did...

As I walked to my next class, conversations and laughter floated all around me, but no laughter could penetrate the pain of my own misery. Gym class was next. I hated gym.

The big gym with its bright lights and tan floor smelled like basketballs and body odor. Thank goodness, a cool breeze blew down from fans on the high ceiling. I crossed my arms in front of me and peered around the room. There were only three girls besides me, and they were all "popular."

While changing in the locker room, I had heard them giggling and felt sure they were laughing about me and my skinny, awkward body. As I stood next to them in the gym, my face turned crimson just thinking about their taunts and this miserable class. I prayed there would be other girls coming out of the locker room. It couldn't be just the four of us girls with all these boys!

The gym teacher started class. "We are going to split into teams for basketball. Captains are Lee, John, and Mark."

Team captains began selecting kids for their teams. Non-athletic types, like me, looked down at the floor, twisting their feet.

I glanced across the gym and saw a boy mocking me. He pushed his knees together, making them touch; put his head down; and crossed his arms in front of him. He looked right at me when he did it.

I was horrified. I knew my skinny legs turned in and my knees touched. *I hate my legs!*

Flames burned under my skin. I wanted to run outside and all the way home. Too bad I lived ten miles out of town. I stayed, unwillingly, shoving the tears that threatened to surface deep down into my gut.

I missed a lot of school in 9th grade, especially on the days I had gym. The avoidance made gym class much worse when I actually attended. For a while, Mom let me stay home when I claimed to be sick, but eventually she caught on to my tactics and scheduled a meeting with the guidance counselor.

The meeting with the guidance counselor didn't go well because all I could say was "I don't know what is wrong." As if that would solve my problems! In writing this book, I talked to Mom about 9th grade and how I missed so much school. She said I was so afraid to go to school that she thought I had been raped! She couldn't get me to open up no matter how often she pressed me for information.

The avoidance of school, dropping out of choir, and my unwillingness to talk about my fears with anyone were the turning points. Shyness transformed into social anxiety disorder. Outwardly, I may have seemed the same, but inside the pain I experienced was even worse. The number of embarrassing situations I relived in my mind and the negative self-talk that was running rampant every minute of every day was physically and emotionally exhausting. The Secret Pain was eating me alive. It was uncontrollable. In high school, everyone is just trying to fit in, to be confident and popular. Kids with issues like mine take criticism to heart and are unable to forget even unintentional slights. Maybe I was so hard on myself because deep in my heart I wanted to be outgoing, relaxed and friendly. The Secret Pain would not let me be who I truly wanted to be. I always thought that people must have been able to tell I was shy by the way I acted and the way I looked, but surprisingly, many years later, when talking to former classmates, I discovered that people thought I was anti-social and unfriendly. If people only knew what was really going in my head!

I can't stress how important it is to communicate. Ask for help! Don't assume that people can read your mind – because they can't! Just as my classmates assumed of me, people may think that you are unfriendly or anti-social. Never be ashamed of SAD. It is a disorder that can happen to anyone. Talk to a guidance counselor, teacher, parent, or trusted friend. If the advice you are getting doesn't feel right to you, talk to someone else. True friends and family will be sympathetic and understanding; they will not judge you. People who are not supportive are not true friends. Remember, God is there for you. He puts people in your life for a reason. Trust in God, pray for help, and help will arrive. But – you need to do your part and open up.

Think of a person you want to be like. What qualities of that person would you like to see in yourself someday?

_____

_____

List five qualities about yourself that you love:

1. _____

2. _____

3. _____

4. _____

5. _____

List three people who you are willing to confide in about your struggles with shyness:

1. _____

2. _____

3. _____

Chapter Four

Struggling to Fit in at School

*"So do not fear, for I am with you; do not be dismayed, for
I am your God. I will strengthen you and help you; I will
uphold you with my righteous right hand."*
– Isaiah 41:10, The New International Version

Some kids just seem to love school and socializing, while others struggle day in and day out wishing for the school day to end. I continued pushing through difficult year after difficult year. Every day was emotionally draining. I would look at those "popular," "snobby" girls, wanting their lives just for one day. I assumed life must have been so easy for them. Now I realize that everyone struggles in some way; the struggles are just different – like all of us. We are all different. God blessed us with challenges, which, although you may not believe it now, make us stronger.

Those girls I once labeled snobby may have simply been hiding their own fears and anxiety. I've learned that we tend to judge others more harshly when we are suffering ourselves.

In sophomore year, I continued to look for ways to dull The Secret Pain. I wondered why it was getting worse instead of better. I had heard adults say that kids would outgrow their shyness. Why wasn't I outgrowing mine? Why did my heart race? Why did my hands tremble? Why did I blush? I prayed to God for help and searched for answers. There had to be a reason for my pain, a reason and a cure.

My early searches led to reading books about raising my self-esteem. I'd read these books in my room, secretly. I didn't want anyone to know that there was something wrong with me. That would be like admitting I was flawed in some way. The books typically focused on getting out there and pushing through the fear. I don't recall reading about identifying, understanding, and changing the negative thoughts that were growing in my mind. I wasn't aware that my thoughts were the root of my problem, or perhaps I didn't want to see the connection as a teenager. As far as I was concerned, I couldn't be causing this intense fear with my own mind; there had to be something else wrong with me.

Life moved on. At sixteen, I got my driver's license, my first job, and a car, all of which added up to no more bus rides! Although the bullying at school had decreased considerably, I was afraid all the time. While sitting in class, I would allow my thoughts to run rampant, feeling like people were looking at me, expecting someone to tease me or simply worrying that I would blush for no apparent reason.

You may wonder how I was able to interview for a job, take a driving test and serve food in a restaurant when I lived with this fear every day. I did it all with The Secret Pain gnawing at my insides.

People don't really see as much of your fear as you think. It's usually those of us who experience the same fear who see the fear in others – that is, when we actually take the time to look at others instead of focusing on ourselves.

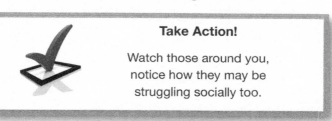

Take Action!

Watch those around you, notice how they may be struggling socially too.

While I experienced emotional pain all the time, I did see some positives in my life. I had a loving family, and two best friends, Sally and Rachel. I felt joy when I would laugh with my family over the silly antics of my siblings. I felt acceptance when Sally, Rachel and I would spend an afternoon in Rachel's bedroom talking about boys and our life dreams.

I believe it's important to have a friend or someone you can confide in. Being alone and having SAD is not a good combination. Although it may be difficult for you, reach out to others and notice when someone is reaching out to you. Take gradual steps to build new friendships and be sure to spend time with the friends you have now. You may not be ready to talk to them about your struggles with SAD, but it can still ease your suffering to be with others who care about you.

What are three situations that are socially challenging for you? Why?

1. _____

2. _____

3. _____

List the name(s) of a person you want to build a friendship with:

_____

_____

Write down a topic you could use to start a conversation with that person. What areas of your life do you have in common?

_____

_____

Learning to drive and working were not the only new activities I added to my life the summer leading up to my junior year. When my friends, Rachel and Sally, somehow persuaded me to have my own sweet sixteen party, I was also introduced to alcohol. I thought maybe, just maybe, a few sips would help me to be less nervous...

August 1985
Sixteen years old

Dirt from the gravel driveway kicked up around my feet as I walked the path from my parents' house to Uncle Paul's. My Uncle Paul had given me permission to have my party at his place. As I looked up at the beautiful sunset, the sky turning to a deep orange-red, I felt a moment of calmness wash over me, but as the sun disappeared and the time of the party drew closer, I felt the old familiar thoughts drift in and dispel any lasting sense of peace...

What if I don't know what to say? What if people are bored? What if no one shows up? What if I do something embarrassing? What if I make a fool of myself? A party is such a stupid idea. What was I THINKING!!??

I walked across the pea-green carpet in Uncle Paul's dining room into the kitchen. Setting a bottle of my mixed-alcohol concoction on the counter, I smiled, knowing I had successfully snuck into my parents' liquor cabinet. Opening the fridge, I double-checked the beer supply.

I grabbed a sixteen-ounce can of Miller Lite and cracked it open, my first taste of alcohol. Taking a big swig, I nearly spit it out. My face crinkled in disgust.

How do people drink this stuff? YUCK!

Choking down the beer, I walked into the living room to make sure everything was in order. I smiled and shook my head at Uncle Paul's bachelor-style living room. A pool table occupied most of the room.

Rachel and Sally were the first to arrive. Sally noticed that I had already finished a can of beer. "Getting the party started early?" she asked.

"Yeah, I'm a little nervous and thought maybe this would help me calm down."

Music blared out of the stereo. People started flowing in: five, ten, fifteen. Laughter and loud voices mixed with the music as cigarette smoke hovered everywhere.

I don't know what to say to people. Everyone is looking at me. I must've been insane to agree to this party.

I stayed close to Sally and Rachel at first. I guzzled more beer and started drinking and sharing the alcohol concoction I now called "combat juice."

Conversations flowed more smoothly once I was officially drunk. I passed the combat juice around and made sure everyone had a beer. I became the perfect hostess and, for a brief time, felt confident.

A short while later, I wobbled over to Rachel. "The room is sp... sp... spinning. I'm not feeling too good." I clasped my stomach with my hand. "I'm gonna lie down a while." My words slurred together. I struggled to stand.

Rachel walked me to Uncle Paul's bedroom and let me pass out on the bed.

A few hours later, I rolled over. Squeezing my eyes together, I placed my hand on my throbbing forehead. I nearly gagged, the taste of stale beer coating the inside of my mouth. Muffled voices and music filtered under the door.

I flipped my legs over the side of the bed and pushed my body up with my hands. Glancing in the mirror on the nearby dresser, I attempted to adjust my hair. My throbbing head drew me back toward the bed, but I knew I would miss the entire party if I didn't get up.

I peered into the living room. "Hi guys. Did I miss much?"

I was greeted with laughter and kind-hearted teasing. I found a place to sit near Rachel and Sally. My face turned red with embarrassment remembering my drunken condition earlier in the night, but no one seemed to notice.

Rachel and Sally filled me in on everything I missed: who came and went, who threw up from drinking too much, who spilled an entire pitcher of beer on the pool table.

The house was a disaster.

Sally, being the motherly type, felt she needed to take care of me. "Lisa, you need to eat." She handed me a paper plate with a slice of pizza.

I nearly threw up just looking at the pizza, but I managed to take a bite. Immediately my stomach flipped and I threw up on the pizza in front of everyone. The pizza flew off the paper plate and onto the floor. Laughter erupted around me. I wanted to crawl into a hole.

Rachel and Sally each grabbed an arm and walked me into the bathroom to clean me up.

Wearing an embarrassed smile, I rejoined the party once again and the post-drunk buzz helped me to socialize with people at the party until it wrapped up in the wee hours of the morning.

The next day, the devastation, the shame, and the added embarrassment of not remembering everything I had done or said only doubled my fears and symptoms of SAD. While I was drinking, it was fine, but afterward the pain was unbearable.

I can assure you, DRINKING IS NOT THE ANSWER! According to the Anxiety Disorders Association of America, about 20 percent of people with social anxiety disorder also suffer from alcohol abuse or dependence (Anxiety Disorders Association of America). Drinking seemed like it made things easier. It relaxed me. I had this newfound confidence. It was almost like I had another personality – the "partying Lisa" instead of the "shy Lisa."

When I was drunk, I was able to mask SAD and act like the outgoing social butterfly I truly wanted to be. My naïve mind thought that alcohol could help me, yet the drinking also made the times that didn't involve alcohol even harder. I acted more outgoing with alcohol and then acted like my shy self again without it. People didn't realize that the only time I was even close to being outgoing was when I was in a drunken stupor. Although there were some negative consequences, I quickly latched on to alcohol as a solution for socializing outside of school. I became a member of a clique: the "partying clique."

Falsely believing that alcohol could help me actually delayed my healing. The Secret Pain was getting worse. Embarrassing experiences like puking on the pizza at my sweet sixteen party added fuel to the fire when the teasing drew more attention toward me. I was blushing so often that my face must have been red continuously!

On the work front, I struggled in my role as a cashier at a fast food restaurant. It was at that job that I started to realize I was more embarrassed around people I knew. A friend would walk into the restaurant and I would feel my face and neck heat up. Usually no one said anything to me about my red face. I'm sure they must have noticed – how could a person miss a face as red as the stop sign on the street corner? Maybe people didn't notice. Maybe my face wasn't really red. Maybe if I hadn't blathered on about my life over a few beers, I wouldn't have had a reason to be embarrassed.

I never understood why I was more flustered around friends. Normal people would be embarrassed around strangers. Aren't friends supposed to be safe?

Do you find yourself trying to figure out rational reasons why you are embarrassed in one situation or another? There may not be an answer, but I do know that your thoughts have a LOT to do with it.

See if you can hear your thoughts when you get embarrassed.

Do you know what's going on in your head when you get embarrassed? Stop and listen. See if you can hear the thoughts. It does take some practice, but it's the first step toward changing and understanding yourself. Just begin by noticing your thoughts. You can even write them down in a journal for your eyes only.

You may notice that your thoughts are often about comparing yourself to others and not measuring up. Remember you are your own person. You will be more like your true self once the anxious thoughts get out of your way. Understanding social anxiety disorder and how to overcome it is the key to your success. You will be able to get through this! Your life might seem difficult now, but I PROMISE YOU it will get better. Instead of latching onto the wrong solutions like I did with alcohol, you can learn to enjoy your life NOW in the present. You are on your way. You are beginning to heal.

What thoughts are running through your mind when you get embarrassed socially?

1. _____

2. _____

3. _____

What solutions have you tried that you know aren't good for you? What will you do to change?

_____

_____

This school year, as your healing progresses, what one goal will you set for trying something new?

_____

_____

_____

Chapter Five

The Dating Scene

*"Lifting the veil of fear allows us to see the love around us
and how we as individuals can touch others."*
- Jessie O'Neill

My life changed even more in junior year when I started dating. Eddie teased me about puking on the pizza at my sweet sixteen party and laughed at my crimson face when he saw that he successfully embarrassed me. I found out later from Rachel that Eddie liked me and wanted to ask me out. He sure had a strange way of showing his interest!

Eddie was two years younger than me. He had thick black hair that was messy, but cute. His smile always made him look like he was up to something. It was hard to believe he was a freshman!

September 1985
Sixteen years old, Junior year

Mixed emotions flashed through my mind while getting ready for my first date with Eddie: first excitement, then nervousness, then happiness, then worry. *I can't believe I'm going on a date! My stomach is doing flips. How will I know what to say? Will he try to kiss me?*

Mom gave me a hug on my way out the door and told me to be careful. She seemed to have mixed emotions, too. She said she was happy for me, but she seemed worried. I thought it must be normal for a mom to feel anxious about her oldest daughter's first date.

I knew Mom would worry even more if I told her I was nervous, so I acted like it was no big deal. Instead, I shared my worries with Sally and Rachel. Familiar worries about how I looked and what I would say were now accentuated with new worries about the first date. How was I supposed to act on a date with a boy? Would Eddie try to hold my hand? Would he be discouraged by how insecure I would surely appear to be? Would he ever ask me out again? Sally and Rachel tried reassuring me that the date would go okay, but while I appreciated their support, it didn't take away my anxiety.

I drove to Eddie's house to pick him up. He was only fourteen, and I was the one with the license and car. We sat in silence during the awkward ten-minute drive to the theater. Eddie sat next to me, occasionally glancing over.

The lights in the movie theater highlighted the red walls. Once our eyes adjusted to the dim lighting, we pushed down the creaky, cushy seats and sat down.

The knots in my stomach tightened. I rubbed my sweaty hands on my jeans, took a deep breath, and drank some Diet Pepsi to moisten my dry mouth. Unsure of what to say, I reached over and shoved a handful of popcorn in my mouth.

Eddie broke the silence. "I don't know about you, but I'm really nervous!"

I felt myself relax a little knowing that, for once, someone else was also nervous!

"I'm nervous, too," I admitted.

My anxiousness lessened as the night went on. Eddie put me at ease. I found he was easy to talk to, especially in the darkness surrounding us in the theater and later as we sat in my car in his driveway. Any glimpse of my nervousness wasn't as noticeable in the darkness.

Eddie and I talked about our friends and the movie, neither one of us wanting the night to end. I looked over; Eddie fidgeted with the button on his red flannel shirt. He looked at me with his deep brown eyes, leaned over and placed his lips gently on mine.

A deep-rooted desire rose to the surface. Desperately needing to feel wanted and beautiful, I returned the kiss with an unexpected passion.

Our first kiss.

On my way home, I felt all warm inside thinking about Eddie: his smile, his deep voice, and those very telling eyes. The kiss. A blush covered my face thinking about the kiss. The date and Eddie's affection made me realize how badly I had needed the self-esteem-building attention. My heart felt different – lighter, happier. At the time I thought this was what self-esteem was all about – someone like Eddie liking me. At the time, I didn't realize how far from the truth this really was.

The relationship with Eddie took off quickly. Eddie gave me the security I desperately needed. He always acted goofy and joked around so everyone focused their attention on him rather than on me, for once in my life. We spent as much time together as we could. We were an "item." Better yet, any remnants of bullying stopped once I started dating Eddie. It was a miracle.

Eddie was the answer to my prayers. The intensity of The Secret Pain would loosen its grip when he put his arm around me or held my hand.

Desperate to overcome The Secret Pain, I latched onto Eddie with both hands. I needed him and I believed he needed me, but I soon learned differently...

April 1986
Eight months with Eddie

Sitting at a fast food restaurant, I reached for one of Eddie's French fries and savored the crisp saltiness in my mouth before washing it down with a swig of Diet Coke.

Earlier that day, Eddie had told me that he wanted to talk about something at lunch. Now, I looked at Eddie in anticipation. He finally blurted out, "I'm going to visit my mom for the summer." Eddie lived with his grandma and his mom lived ten hours away.

It was April 1 and, being a jokester, Eddie had played various April Fool's Day jokes on me that entire week. I laughed, "Yeah, right! April Fool's to me."

"I'm not joking," Eddie said.

My smile faded when Eddie didn't return a smile, but rather a frown and concerned eyes. He wasn't kidding. My heart felt like it had stopped beating.

"I'm leaving as soon as school is out," Eddie said while taking a bite of his quarter-pounder.

It seemed like forever before I was able to talk. "For the entire summer? You can't leave me here alone!" I cried.

"Lisa, you know how rarely I get to see my mom."

I knew this trip to his mom's was important to him, but it didn't matter. "I can't make it without you here! I need you!"

Eddie let out a frustrated sigh and rolled his eyes. "Geez Lisa, come on! It's just for the summer. You can hang out with Sally and Rachel."

Eddie tried to act like he didn't care about being away from his mom and his grade school friends, but he didn't fool me. I knew he was a lost soul, looking for some reassurance that he was worthy of being loved – truly loved. He needed his mom, yet I couldn't allow myself to think of his needs, not when I needed him so much more.

I reached over and placed my hand on Eddie's; tears ran down my cheeks. "Please don't do this," I begged.

Eddie grabbed the fast food tray and stood up. "It's not like I'm leaving forever. It's only for a few months."

We needed to go back to school. I wiped my tears and blew my nose in a napkin. We drove back to school in silence, my thoughts filling the void: *How am I going to be able to make it without Eddie here for the WHOLE summer? I feel so safe when I'm with him. Eddie helps me to feel more sure of myself. All of that is going to change when he leaves. I know my life will be miserable…*

Sally had often told me that I was getting too serious with Eddie too quickly. She said I should live my own life, not have it revolve around Eddie. I listened to her, but I never really heard her.

That day when Eddie told me he was leaving for the summer, I realized Sally might be right. I was dependent on Eddie and relied on him to build up my confidence.

It is important to maintain friendships even when you are in a relationship. Although it might be difficult to hear what your friends have to say when you are in the passion of love, they will usually, if they are true friends, tell you the truth. They will tell you when you are becoming too attached to your boyfriend or girlfriend and losing balance in your life. Your friends can see what is really happening in your relationship.

Your friends can see what is really happening in your relationship.

Even if you may not agree, at least listen and think about what your friends are telling you. They may be right! Open your heart and listen.

Take Action!

Make plans to do something with a friend.

When Eddie left that first summer, I went out with Sally and Rachel. My drinking continued to increase on the weekends when the partying Lisa came out. I filled the void of Eddie with a new guy named Brad, whom I met at a party. I was devoted to Eddie, but the loneliness I felt when he was gone was more than I could take. When I was with Brad, I felt safe and comfortable and, for the first time since Eddie left, happy. I felt guilty about Brad, but a few drinks washed away the guilt. Brad and alcohol mixed well.

Eddie came back and we had our ups and downs. He never found out about Brad, surprisingly, even though we lived in a town of only 3,000 people, but our relationship never went back to the way it was before he left. The distance between us over the summer changed our relationship. It wasn't easy to stay in touch when he was gone. There were no cell phones, no Internet. Just a plain old telephone. Today, with texting and the Internet, it's easier to stay in touch during a long-distance romance.

If you are in a relationship, be careful not have your life revolve around your significant other. I learned that using a relationship as a "fix" for SAD or any other issue only makes the problem worse in the long run. As with alcohol, dependency on a boyfriend or girlfriend will only delay the healing process. Putting so much pressure on your partner and needing him or her to be there for you all the time – to never leave you – is an unreasonable and unhealthy expectation. In my case, as a desperate sixteen-year-old, I was putting that much pressure on a fourteen-year-old! Sure, I loved Eddie, but part of the reason why we stayed together for so long was because I was so dependent on him.

It might be time to take a look at your relationship and decide if you are together simply because you need a guy or girl by your side, or if you really, truly do love that person and see yourself marrying him or her some day. It's time to think about yourself and what you need to do to heal.

What are you doing to maintain independence even if you are in a serious relationship?

_____

_____

What advice are your friends giving you as it pertains to your relationship? Might their advice be accurate?

_____

_____

What activities do you continue to do with your friends even though you are in a relationship?

_____

_____

Part Two

Coping with the Pain

Chapter Six

Dealing with College Life

"The very least you can do in your life is to figure out what you hope for. And the most you can do is live inside that hope. Not admire it from a distance but live right in it, under its roof."
- Barbara Kingsolver

Graduating from high school felt wonderful! After graduation, I looked back on high school as a miserable time in my life. I never wanted to go back. It always seemed like I had never measured up to the popular crowds. If it hadn't been for Rachel, Sally and Eddie, I don't think I would have made it through. However, sitting here today, as a 42-year-old, I have to admit that there are definitely some positive memories. What pains me is that if I hadn't allowed fear to overpower me, I could've had a much better experience. This is what I wish for you and know that you can have. With support and practice you can learn to overcome your Secret Pain.

After graduation, I moved to the big city of Milwaukee (a two-hour drive from my small hometown) and attended Patricia Stevens Career College and Finishing School. The all-girls school touted an educational program that would increase my confidence and give me the secretarial skills I needed to obtain a job immediately after graduation. Eddie and I were still together, so I came home every weekend to see him.

I shared a room with two girls whom I had never met before. My anxiety grew when I realized the living room was also my bedroom! My bed was the shared couch. I was in the center of everything and had no privacy. Being socially challenged, I struggled to build a friendship with my roommates. One of the roommates and I didn't get along at all. College life was doomed to be miserable too, I thought.

Then, another girl at school, Donna, reached out to me in friendship. When I told Donna about my roommate situation, she suggested that I move in with her because her roommate had moved out. To my surprise, I was able to communicate with the right people and ask for a change.

The living arrangements were just one facet of my college life that proved challenging. The other difficult aspect was dealing with college classes. The struggles I had had in high school were minor compared to the expectations teachers placed on students in my college courses. I worked outside of my comfort zone every day, stretching my limits as I dealt with constant change, new people, and new challenges. A class dedicated solely to speeches terrified me! To top it off, the finishing portion of the college, which was similar to modeling, included classes like visual poise!

August 1987
Eighteen years old

We stood in a line, decked out in the school dress code – appropriate dresses (six inches below the knee), high heels, and hair pulled in a bun.

"Students, let's take turns practicing walking and turning on stage," the visual poise teacher announced.

The Secret Pain burned inside of me, flames of heat shooting through every organ and limb. *Stupid! STUPID IDIOT! I can feel my face heating up already and I'm not even on stage yet. Worse yet, I have my hair up and everyone will see my bright red face.* I glanced into the mirror, casually adjusting my hair as if I wasn't dying on the inside.

I walked carefully up the stairs and on to the stage, my shaky legs teetering in high heels; my damp, trembling hands at my side; and a fake smile painted across my face. *It's hopeless. Everyone is going to see me make a fool of myself. Here I go, walking into misery…*

The room was filled with mirrors and I saw myself: bright red face, neck, and ears; my stick ankles shaking in my high-heeled shoes; and, behind me, everyone's eyes locked on me. My worst nightmare was coming true. Everyone saw me exactly as I felt: weak, anxious, and afraid.

Walking out of the visual poise class, I hung my head low and made my way reluctantly to speech class. When I first saw that speech class was a required college credit, my entire body tensed. Now, it was time for the dreaded class; there was no way to avoid it.

I sat behind my desk, bending the note cards with my sweaty hands. Before she selected the first speaker, the teacher explained that eye contact and vocal variety were very important. Every time the teacher looked around the room to pick the next lucky speaker, I felt my anxiety level rise.

When my turn arrived, I gathered my note cards and pushed myself up from the desk with trembling hands in an attempt to support my shaky legs. Walking to the podium, I felt as if quicksand covered the floor.

Once at the podium, I was unable to catch my breath or make eye contact. As sweat poured down my back, I creased the note cards in my hands. While reading my notes, I felt like I might collapse to the floor. Eventually, the anxiety reduced a little and somehow I managed to finish the speech.

The teacher said, "Thank you, Lisa. Next time you need to work on eye contact, but overall I could tell you were very well prepared."

I can't believe how horrible I did! Everyone just had to see my hands shaking! I just keep messing up everything...

Experiences like this were the norm during college. I was extremely hard on myself and failed to realize that other girls had the same fears. There was no way for me to see that others were struggling because I was so closed in by my own insecurity. Maybe they were just better at hiding it. Desperate to minimize my embarrassment, the need for perfection and control grew. I had hoped that college would increase my confidence, but how could it when The Secret Pain kept haunting me day in and day out? I wanted to be outgoing, normal – like everyone else. My prayers became more desperate, asking God to help me be emotionally strong and pleading for some reprieve from the person I felt

I was becoming: a nervous wreck on the verge of a breakdown.

In college, you need to take care of yourself. College is hard enough without setting unrealistic expectations about being perfect and in control. Burdening yourself in this way will make college unbearable. Be careful, because while these are good traits to have in certain circumstances, they will not help you to heal from SAD. If you put too much pressure on yourself, you will only increase your stress and anxiety levels.

The drinking I had been doing during high school continued when I went home on weekends. Eddie and I would spend as much time together as we could, although it felt different. The fact that we were only together on Saturdays and Sundays weakened our relationship. I wrote him letters and we talked on the phone once in a while, but I missed him terribly. I wondered if he missed me too. He may have enjoyed his freedom since I had been dating him since he was fourteen. I sometimes feared he might enjoy it too much, and soon my fear became a reality...

March 1988
Nineteen years old, over two years with Eddie

Gravel popped under my tires as I pulled into the driveway for a party at Eddie's classmate's house.

My concerns about Eddie and our relationship continued to grow. Eddie seemed like he was distancing himself from me more each day.

I parked the car and looked over at Eddie, "You know I love you with all my heart, don't you?"

Eddie let out a frustrated sigh. "Yeah, I love you too. Can't we just go inside?"

My stomach tensed. "Is everything okay with us, Eddie?"

Eddie glanced down. "I don't know."

"What do you mean 'you don't know'?"

"It doesn't feel right anymore. "

I held my breath.

Eddie continued, "I think we should break up."

No words could escape my mouth.

"It's been over two years now. It's time to move on."

I finally found my voice. "Oh Eddie, how can you do this to me? I love you so much. I need you in my life." Thoughts of Eddie with someone else made me sick to stomach.

"You will be okay," he assured me. "You are starting a new job soon and will make new friends." Eddie reached over and gently slid his hand across my tear-stained cheek, "I do love you. You deserve more out of your life than what I can give you right now."

"Please don't do this to me! I can give you more space. I can stop being so needy. I just don't want us to be over," I pleaded.

"It's over." Eddie looked down in despair.

I still remember the song that played on the radio when Eddie broke my heart. I had the opportunity to talk to Eddie recently, and to my surprise, he remembers the song, too. The song, Whitesnake's "Here I Go Again," made me think of Eddie's life. *Here I go again on my own. Goin' down the only road I've ever known. Like a drifter I was born to walk alone...* (Coverdale)

Sadness grew. I wondered if Eddie would be okay. Did he really want this, or was he pushing me away because he thought it was best for me? Didn't he know he needed me as much as I needed him? Like the song, he was a drifter. He moved away from his mom to live with extended family. He was a loner trying to fit into a family – my family.

I wiped my tears and glanced up at Eddie with red puffy eyes. Eddie leaned over, as he did on our first date, and gently kissed me.

Our last kiss.

First love. Heartbreak.

The break-up seemed so devastating at the time, but honestly, I think I was ready to move on, too. Eddie had to be the one to end the relationship because my severe dependence on having a boyfriend wouldn't have allowed me to break up with him. While I was with Eddie, I felt like I couldn't live life without him, but, after the break-up, I managed to survive. I fueled my dependence on boyfriends by dating guys who filled the Eddie void. Was it Eddie I missed, or having a boyfriend? Likely, it was a little of both. If I would have been confident enough in myself, I could have maintained some level of independence and enjoyed the single life for a while.

The guidance I will give you about relationships is that being single can be a good thing. It teaches you about yourself and what you want out of life. You will have the opportunity to spend more time with your friends, find yourself, and enjoy your independence.

The friendships I had with Sally and Rachel stayed strong. I wrote them letters while away at college, which helped me to stay connected. Sally and I got together on weekends. We did a good job keeping up with our underage drinking activities at beer parties in a farmer's woods or at a friend's country farmhouse. Rachel started going to a college in Milwaukee three months after I started at Patricia

Stevens (which was also in Milwaukee), although we only saw each other a few times during the time we lived there.

While The Secret Pain was with me every day, it did seem like the college experience helped me to become a little more confident. Could it be that my prayers for confidence were finally answered? Would this confidence continue to grow?

If you are in college or going to college soon, take advantage of the time you are there. Enjoy your weekends on the college campus. Participate in extracur-

Your motivation to overcome SAD will drive you toward a life filled with positive experiences.

ricular activities. Meet new people! You may need to make gradual efforts as you heal from SAD, but it will be possible over time. Your motivation to overcome SAD will drive you toward a life filled with positive experiences rather than a life filled with fear.

List a goal you recently set – and met – that helped you to feel more confident:

_____

_____

What will you do to make sure you don't allow perfection and control to rule your college life?

_____

_____

What type of extracurricular activities might you look into at college?

_____

_____

What new goal will you set and achieve that will help you reduce your anxiety?

_____

_____

Chapter Seven

Perfection and Control at Work: Friend or Foe?

"In the confrontation between the stream and the rock,
the stream always wins –
not through strength but by perseverance."
- H. Jackson Brown

Once I finished college, I started interviewing. It was frightening for me, but I understood that most people are nervous during interviews. Luckily, college provided me with a little confidence and a good understanding of the interview process. It also lived up to its promise of job placement; I was hired as a secretary for a sales company right out of school. With a chance to start anew, I was determined to let everyone see the confident Lisa: the woman who was sure of herself and at ease with life. As you may expect, it wasn't quite that easy. When I walked in on my first day, my stomach was a ball of nerves. Realizing that my desk was the first thing people would see when they walked in made me even more frazzled.

As with every new experience, my newfound employment triggered frequent bouts of The Secret Pain, so I developed a few mechanisms to help me cope. First, my old friends, "perfection" and "control," came in handy. I allowed myself no mistakes. A mistake would be embarrassing, and I tried very hard to be perfect. I discovered that certain people caused more anxiety than others. Although I didn't know why, this fact gave me some control. Whenever possible, I steered clear of these people.

My new friends, "acting really busy" and "directing attention away from my face," were proving valuable, too. To deal with the location of my desk, I would immerse myself in what was happening on my computer screen and "act really busy." When clients arrived in the office, I would greet them but would then grab a notepad to jot down their names in an effort to "direct attention away from my face."

Dealing with the outgoing, high-intensity personalities of the sales people in the office was both good and bad. The sales people liked attention, which was good, because then attention was taken away from me. But when the sales people communicated with me, the direct eye contact and high-energy conversations proved to be a bit challenging...

May 1988
Nineteen years old
Three months in the job

"This client is very demanding. We need to impress, impress, impress," said Steve as he handed off some sales updates to me.

Steve's red, out-of-control hair mirrored his intensity. His hands moved quickly as he explained what he needed done.

I looked down at the changes Steve noted, tipping my head enough so my hair covered the sides of my face. As Steve continued, I pointed my pen down on the paper to draw Steve's attention away from me.

Seeing this as a great opportunity to be really busy so that people wouldn't talk to me unexpectedly in the office, I committed to finishing the updates within an hour.

I directed my attention to the computer screen, closed my mind to whatever was going on around me, and focused on the work. This type of coping behavior gave me the ability to produce high quality work quickly.

I sometimes wondered whether these coping techniques would reduce the bouts of The Secret Pain or make them worse in the long run, but I didn't allow myself to dwell on it because the techniques seemed to be helping for the time being.

As you prepare to move into a career or investigate career changes, be sure and research all of your options. Challenge yourself to think outside of your comfort zone.

You can do more than you think you can! If a certain career is appealing and energizing to you one minute but frightening the next, remember that SAD may be planting doubts in your mind. This career that energizes you may be your destiny, but it may not be your destiny until after you have started healing from SAD. Once you begin to heal, don't let anything or anyone stop you from doing what you love.

Take Action!

Investigate career
options today!

When you are at the point where you have identified some career options and are ready to interview, talk to people who can help you prepare, such as a parent or a teacher. Sometimes people don't prepare for an interview at all – that's a mistake, especially if you have SAD. Being prepared isn't a bad thing in this circumstance. It will not only help to reduce your anxiety but also increase your odds of being hired. Research the company. Write down ideas about what you could discuss to show you are qualified for the position. Write down any questions you have for the interviewer. Bring the notes and questions with you into the interview. If you have pertinent examples of any of your work from a school project or a previous job, bring those along, too.

Once you land a job, be realistic in the expectations you set for yourself. Everyone needs time to adjust and learn, even people without SAD. If you have extreme difficulty communicating with others, SAD may have a negative impact on your career right now. It's okay. Don't be discouraged; you will get past this. Take slow and steady steps to heal and you will see positive changes in your career.

Alternatively, if you are attached to perfection and control like I was, these qualities could benefit your career, but negatively impact your health. It really depends on your symptoms and the coping mechanisms you are using to survive. In my case, I was very self-aware. I could be quite hard on myself when it came to my work performance. And although the flames of anxiety were always burning, sometimes red hot at the core, the sales people said I was reliable and efficient. It felt good to see that my efforts to be perfect and in control were benefiting me. What I didn't know at the time was that the stress I put on myself would result in many health issues as my career progressed.

What type of career interests you? Why?

_____

_____

_____

What concerns do you have about this career choice?
How will you address your concerns?

_____

_____

_____

Who can you confide in when you begin interviewing
for a job?

_____

_____

What qualities do you have that could benefit you
when you start a new career?

_____

_____

_____

What is one step you can take now to begin planning
for a new career?

_____

A year after I started my first job at the sales company, I landed a new secretarial position at a paper company. I set my expectations high again. Even though I never believed I looked like the "confident Lisa" at my previous job, I hoped that would change at the new job. My new wish was that people would see me as a confident, hard-working employee who spoke up at meetings. This new company was much larger and had its share of challenges for me, from new people, to unplanned discussions, to really long hallways (which I hated!). The Secret Pain hung on like a virus, making even simple social interactions emotionally exhausting...

May 1989
Twenty years old
Three months at new job

I threw myself into my work once again, taking on more than I could handle in an attempt to keep the negative thoughts at bay. I told myself that if I stayed busy, people wouldn't try to talk to me.

One day, even I realized I needed a break from my work, so I mustered up the courage to stop by Sara's desk to chat. I pushed myself up out of my chair and started walking down the long hallway. Doubt about this anxiety-producing move followed me like a black cloud. *I'm bothering her. She probably doesn't have time to talk to me.*

The Secret Pain boiled up to the surface. *Crap. Here I go again. Sara is my friend, I shouldn't be nervous about talking to her. But I'm sure I will say something stupid and embarrass myself.*

I pivoted around and returned to my desk.

Despair.

I let out a frustrated sigh and acted like I was looking for something on my desk. *There. Better. For crying out loud, can't anything be easy in my life?*

Then I did something brave. I decided to ignore The Secret Pain for just one moment and I walked over to Sara's desk. "Hey Sara, how's it going?" I talked a mile a minute because when I was the one talking, the negativity in my mind wasn't so loud. I shared stories about my sisters and friends and I can't even recall if Sara shared anything.

Walking back to my desk, the one-sided conversation with Sara played back in my mind. *Why do I have to talk non-stop? Why can't I remember that Sara might have something to say, too?*

"Hi Lisa! How are you?"

I didn't see the co-worker approaching as I walked back to my desk. The unexpected interruption startled me and painful anxiety rose to the surface, my face instantly turning red.

The co-worker continued, "Wow! Looks like you got some sun!"

Humiliation.

Horror.

Oh my God, he can really tell that I'm blushing. I haven't gotten any sun; I'm white as a ghost. My face is completely red and he noticed it.

The co-worker continued to walk next to me, waiting for my response. I giggled nervously and said, "Yup."

I bee-lined for the closest possible exit, the restroom.

I knew people could tell I was embarrassed. I knew it. I have to control the blushing. This is so embarrassing just thinking about it. He wouldn't have thought I was blushing because a normal person doesn't blush for no reason – like me. I'm the strange one.

In order to gain more control over my environment at the new company, I added a few new coping techniques to my toolkit. I walked fast and always appeared to be in a hurry. Too busy. No time for chatter. I usually carried something, too. If someone tried talking to me, I could act way too interested in what I was holding. Escape routes were carefully planned and long hallways were avoided at all costs.

Because I was so swept up in what I considered to be just one more embarrassing episode in my life, I didn't even realize I had done something that I thought was impossible. I had overruled The Secret Pain! I had successfully ignored the negative voices in my head and talked to Sara anyway.

I never knew at this point in my life that I could simply become aware of my thoughts, but not allow them to impact my body. This concept may not sound achievable to you at this point in your healing process. That's okay. Once you read the therapy techniques discussed in later chapters, you will see that it's important to start at the ground level with therapies and gradually increase your healing strategies.

What type of techniques do you use to cope with SAD?

_____

_____

List three positive thoughts you can tell yourself when you are going into an uncomfortable social situation:

1. _____

2. _____

3. _____

What situation have you been in recently where you ignored the negative voices in your head and pushed forward? What was one positive outcome of this situation?

_____

_____

_____

_____

My career progressed along. At this point, I still hadn't been diagnosed with SAD. In the midst of my social fears, I continued to want more out of my career. I started taking night classes to pursue a degree in business administration. Not only did I move to yet another new large company, but I also continued to change positions within the company, which gave me new environments to adapt to, new people to interact with, and new job responsibilities. Why did I keep pushing forward even though The Secret Pain had so much control over me? Maybe I was a glutton for punishment. Or was it that deep down, beneath the fear, I knew there was a confident, intelligent Lisa, and I fought for her right to thrive, even if I wasn't always aware of it.

After I completed a few college classes, I moved into a computer support job. It worked out pretty well, because I could talk on the phone all day with limited face-to-face interaction with my co-workers. This worked for a while, but in my heart, I wanted more. The standards I set for myself continued to be high. Making a mistake would be very embarrassing and draw undesired attention my way, so I became hyper-vigilant when it came to my work.

A few months into the computer support job, my manager noticed I was very organized and efficient and asked me to manage a project. This meant that I would be leading face-to-face meetings and holding people accountable for delivering tasks. This would be quite a change from sitting behind the telephone helping customers with computer issues...

September 1996
Twenty-seven years old

I glanced up from the project plan and looked cautiously at Matt. "How is everything going with your part of the project, Matt? Are you on target with dates?"

Any shred of confidence I had shown while leading the meeting went out the window when Matt clamored on about the roadblocks with his project work.

Anxiety rush. Blood pumping rapidly through my body.

Why is Matt staring at me? I just asked him a question, why doesn't he address the entire group? Now EVERYONE is looking at me! What is going on? I felt fine a minute ago when I asked Matt the question.

Matt finished talking. Somehow, I managed to take notes while my mind was careening down the anxiety roller-coaster. It was as if I was outside of myself, watching myself take notes.

"Thanks, everyone. That's all for now. I will send out meeting notes in the next day or two."

Running these meetings is the worst experience I have ever had in my life. Everyone keeps looking at me. I bet they are back at their desks right now joking about how socially incompetent I am.

I plopped into the chair at my desk, my heart still beating wildly. I leaned over my notes, placing my hands over my eyes and taking a few deep breaths to regain my composure.

That night, I prayed: *God, I'm feeling very stressed at work and the anxiety rushes seem to be happening more each day. Isn't there anything you can do for me to help make my days easier? Why does misery always need to be a part of my day?*

If you are already in the workforce, remember that it's important to manage your stress level. If you are naturally anxious, stress will exaggerate your symptoms. Stress causes adrenaline levels to spike, and an influx of adrenaline causes anxiety. The combination is toxic for a person with SAD. In my case, I was rushing around, acting really busy, moving fast – that alone would spike my anxiety.

Find out what your triggers are so you can start to understand what's happening. It could be certain people or certain activities that stress you out. It could be that the coping mechanisms you use in an attempt to reduce your anxiety are making your anxiety worse. Opening your eyes and being aware will move you in the right direction.

Everything that is happening to you is happening for a reason. The challenges you are faced with now will only make you stronger in the end. Eventually, you will realize how much a teacher, manager, friend, or co-worker impacted your life. Whether the experience was positive or negative, there's some purpose behind it. As I gently evaluated my past during my healing journey, God's plan for me became clearer.

The challenges you are faced with now will only make you stronger in the end.

As you begin to find out more about SAD, you will better understand your past and the disorder. Communication will be an important part of your healing; just be cautious about how widely you communicate right away because many people don't understand the nature of a disorder like SAD. Talk to those you trust. Keep an open mind and see the positives related to the people and opportunities God places in your life.

What are some behavioral actions or coping mechanisms you use in your school or work life that cause undue stress?

_____

_____

What is one thing you can do in the coming weeks to reduce your stress level?

_____

What are steps you can take to manage your stress on an on-going basis?

_____

_____

How will you keep the career expectations you set for yourself in check?

_____

_____

Often times a person with SAD may have a Type A personality or a high-anxiety personality. Unfortunately, I had both of these personality types. The characteristics of these personality traits became more prevalent when I started my career. See if you recognize any of these traits within yourself.

The Type A personality generally lives at a higher stress level:

- They enjoy achievement of goals, with greater enjoyment in achieving more difficult goals. They are thus constantly working hard to achieve these.

- They find it difficult to stop, even when they have achieved goals.

- They feel the pressure of time, constantly working flat-out.

- They are highly competitive and will, if necessary, create competition.

- They hate failure and will work hard to avoid it.

- They are generally pretty fit and often well-educated (a result of their anxiety).
  (Changing Minds)

Along the same lines as Type A, the high-anxiety personality has a few traits worth mentioning:

- High level of creativity and imagination

- Excessive need for approval

- Extremely high expectations of self

- Excessive need to be in control
  (Peurifoy, 2005, p. 8-9)

The opposite of Type A is Type B. Type B personalities generally live at a lower stress level and typically:

- They work steadily, enjoying achievements but not becoming stressed when goals are not achieved.

- When faced with competition, they do not mind losing and either enjoy the game or back down.

- They may be creative and enjoy exploring ideas and concepts.

- They are often reflective, thinking about the outer and inner worlds.
  (Changing Minds)

As it relates to the high-anxiety personality traits, the high level of creativity and imagination for those afflicted with SAD is what helps them conjure up all sorts of irrational thoughts, fears, and expectations related to social situations. People with SAD and a high-anxiety personality excel at scaring themselves. Just think what will happen when SAD is gone and the creativity and imagination can be used for something positive!

The excessive need for approval and high expectation of self tie in with one of the focuses of this chapter: the need to be perfect. For me, it wasn't only about avoiding mistakes, but ensuring that everyone liked me. I readily agreed with most people's opinions because I worried that they wouldn't like me if I disagreed. My self-image was so low that I needed to have the approval of others to feel okay. I put on a confident face, patiently waiting for recognition while inside The Secret Pain was running rampant.

The excessive need to be in control is the second main subject of this chapter. It's important for a person with SAD to know what's coming, what the plan is, and what the reactions of others will be. When the situation doesn't go according to plan, it's a huge catastrophe. It's hard for a socially anxious person to understand that there are multiple ways to do things. If you were to ask anyone I've worked with in the past, they would say I was an obsessive planner. It was always very important for me to prepare for meetings. I'd have every detail scripted out so that I wouldn't be caught off-guard with a question I couldn't answer. Of course, no matter how much I prepared, I still never had all the answers. Only now do I realize that no one can be prepared for everything, nor are we expected to be.

These traits are prevalent in people without SAD, too, and while I have addressed many of my issues with SAD, I would still classify myself as a Type A, high-anxiety personality. But... I'm okay with that. Now that I understand my personality, I take steps to manage my stress level and work expectations.

People with SAD are generally very self-aware and overly critical of themselves. Sure, people may notice certain nuances about us – those things that we believe we need to change – but people don't really notice as much as we think they do. The symptoms are exaggerated in our minds while people around us simply see an employee trying to get the job done.

I want you to consider that it doesn't really matter what people think of you. It's what you think about yourself that matters. And once you accept yourself and love yourself as you are, your life will change for the better. You are your own person and can be the person you truly want to be, in your heart, without a single worry about being judged by others.

Chapter Eight

The Unexplainable Fears in Everyday Life

*"If you put the same amount of energy toward recovery as you put
toward scaring yourself, success is certain!"*
- Lucinda Bassett

A new set of social challenges appeared when I moved
into my adult life. The Secret Pain took hold when I
went out in public – to the grocery store, out to eat,
on a date, or even on a walk in my neighborhood. I didn't
understand why simple daily activities that everyone on our
planet partakes in wreaked so much havoc on my
well-being...

January 1991
Twenty-two years old

As I strolled through the busy mall, the jewelry displays and latest fashions caught my eye. I stopped in a department store to check out the blankets and sheets, but the shoes stopped me in my tracks. *Ooh shoes! Oh, how much I love shoes!* I was busy ogling all the fabulous styles when I glanced up and saw a colleague from work standing nearby.

Oh my God. What am I going to say? I look terrible. I will make a fool of myself if I talk to this person. Where's my escape route?

I looked cautiously around and shot over to the purses where I hid behind a tall display, pretending to be way too interested in nothing.

Whew, avoided that embarrassment.

"Hi, Lisa. I thought that was you."

Panic.

Fear.

Heart racing.

Palms instantly drenched with sweat.

"Having fun shopping?" my co-worker asked.

I forced my frozen mouth to curve into a smile, "Yup," I muttered, and then looked back at the purses on display.

I am so incompetent. Why can't I have a normal conversation? I hate this!

"That's good, glad you are having fun. Nice seeing you, catch you later."

"Yup, bye," I stammered.

I left the mall after that uncomfortable situation and unwillingly went to the grocery store. Now that I was an adult, out on my own, I couldn't avoid the grocery store. I needed food to live.

The wheels on the grocery cart squeaked along the store aisle. Scanning my list, I squinted from the glare of the bright fluorescent lights.

"Hi, Lisa!"

No! I thought. *Not another person from work stopping right next to my cart!*

Run.

Hide.

No escape.

Trapped.

The Secret Pain took over. My trembling legs struggled to hold my body up. The world around me moved quickly, but I was frozen.

"Wow! It looks like you've been tanning, Lisa. Going on a vacation?"

I'm blushing! Oh my God, and she can see it! What do I say? Why do people have to look at me?

I stammered out a response, "Nope, just feeling really hot. I think I might be coming down with something."

Stupid! Stupid! Couldn't I come up with something better than that? She can tell I am lying!

"There's a lot going around, that's for sure. Well, gotta run! Hope you feel better."

I thought about leaving the store after another humiliating interaction, but I really needed groceries. I walked through the store in great trepidation, picking up items and keeping an eye out for others I might know. If I saw them first, I could act like I forgot something and quickly turn down another aisle.

That night I prayed: *God, why do I react like this when I see people I know in the store? It should be a good thing to socialize, to make friends. My heart is racing just thinking about it. Can't you just help me, God? I've been dealing with this for so many years; it makes me so sad and frustrated. I want to be different, but I don't even know where to start. Will you ever help me to find the answer?*

There are a variety of ways in which SAD can impact a person's life. Some people with SAD are more avoidant than others – they have difficulty leaving their home altogether and struggle with most social interactions, while for others, certain events like speeches or large gatherings cause SAD symptoms. The tendency toward avoidance of social situations can result in a pattern of becoming reclusive and socializing over the Internet, rather than getting out into society.

If you choose to use the Internet to stay connected socially, you may find you can be more like your true self – the person without SAD. But that's not always the case either; if you are like me, you may type something, press send, then worry and agonize about it, wondering whether someone might misinterpret what you wrote. And, if the person doesn't respond immediately, you may wonder if she is mad at you! At least on-line the receiver can't see the physical symptoms of SAD, such as trembling hands. Relying on the Internet for a social life will eventually leave you feeling unfulfilled when it comes to relationships though. This is why it's essential that you take steps to overcome SAD, so you can live a fulfilling life.

When SAD ruled my social life, my most visible symptom was blushing (as I'm sure you have noticed by now). Now, I realize that I blushed simply because I told myself I was going to, and then I did! I allowed my mind to control my physical reaction. Blushing was a trigger and a symptom. I thought it made me look weak and drew undue attention. I couldn't control it, or so I thought, and I didn't like not having control. If I would have realized that the blushing itself wasn't that big of a deal, and stopped fighting it, then it may have happened less often.

Some of the other worries I experienced when out in public were forgetting the person's name, saying something stupid, or being embarrassed about what I was buying – like tampons! While other people are engrossed in their shopping lists, a person with SAD strolls through a store filled with anxiety, and even after an embarrassing event is over, she relives it over and over in her mind for days, months, or even years afterward.

Now I know that life can be so much more enjoyable for me and for you. Imagine browsing through the store without a single worry. Right now, take a moment to visualize seeing someone you know, maybe an old friend whom you haven't seen in a long time. See yourself saying hello and having a great conversation. You exchange email addresses and promise to stay in touch. Instead of being filled with regret about the encounter, you are excited about the opportunity God gave you to run into this old friend. That is what you will soon have! Keep going. Take baby steps and know that you are not alone. God is with you.

In what ways do you avoid going out into society?

_____

_____

_____

What worries you when you are walking through a shopping mall or a grocery store?

_____

_____

_____

List three questions you could ask friends or co-workers when you run into them unexpectedly in the store:

1. _____

2. _____

3. _____

Chapter Nine

A Love Life:
Hindering or Helping?

*"The feeling of love is explicit. When you want to see and feel
something new in your life, then flow with the force of love."*
- Tejas Patel

The dependency I had on a boyfriend stayed with me long after the relationship with Eddie ended. Because I did not have any deep-rooted confidence in myself, I was desperate for love.

My desperation resulted in a string of bad boyfriend choices. Immediately after Eddie, I started dating some guys I met at parties in my hometown. When the partying Lisa came out, so did the new desperate Lisa. Just to give you an idea of how bad my choices were, one of my boyfriends ended up in prison for selling drugs a few years after I dated him.

Maybe that's why my parents didn't approve of him.

I was attracted to guys who had problems and treated me badly. I didn't feel I deserved to be treated with respect. Any guy who would have been good for me would have run away after he realized how needy I could be.

After a few short, failed relationships lasting anywhere from one night to a few months, I met Luke. He was a rebel and I fell in love with him instantly. Luke's smile lit up the room and I would often lose myself in his hazel eyes. He had curly wild hair, a mustache, and a rough unkempt exterior. My parents approved of him; they were unaware of his reputation as a rebel who often mixed with the wrong crowds.

Luke and I became serious quickly. We went out to bars and parties often, both of us enjoying our share of alcohol. We had fun together. I felt like he needed me as much as I needed him. I was there to fulfill his every wish. Luckily, he became less of a rebel after we met and moved away from the bad crowds. He had areas of his life that needed changing and he seemed to want to change, so I helped him. I helped him to quit smoking, to get a job, and to be more responsible with his finances. Fixing Luke helped me, too. It cooled the anxious fire burning inside me.

Sally and I remained very close friends, and she tried to be my voice of reason when it came to my boyfriend choices. A few months into my relationship with Luke, I told Sally that I was sure Luke and I would get married (even though he hadn't proposed yet). Sally thought I was rushing it. She saw me heading down the path of severe dependence on Luke. The only time I spent with Sally was on double dates with Luke and her boyfriend. She warned me that I might scare Luke off if I put too much pressure on him, especially since he'd been such a rebel before we started dating.

A few months later, Luke finally gave into my pressure and did ask me to marry him. Of course, I had to loan him the money for the engagement ring. Since I had recently begun saving up for the house Luke and I would have one day, I could easily part with money for an engagement ring. It was the least I could do; after all, we were going to be together forever. Or so I thought...

July 1990
Twenty years old
Dating Luke 1-1/2 years

Luke and I cuddled up in my bed watching television on a Saturday afternoon. Luke seemed especially quiet all day.

I lifted my head and met Luke's eyes. "Is everything OK?" I slid my hand down the side of Luke's stubbly cheek, "You know you can tell me anything." I smiled at Luke, the love I had for him enveloping my heart.

A look of relief covered Luke's face. "Actually, yeah, there is something bothering me."

Luke and I sat up on the bed.

My stomach tightened and my smile faded. "What's going on?"

"I hate this life – sitting here watching TV, going on weekend trips, going out to eat."

My heart turned cold. "What are you saying?"

"I'd rather be working on my car and hanging out with my friends. You are always trying to change me and I don't like it."

"But... I just love you. I love spending time with you. I need you."

Luke glared at me. "I can't be your everything, Lisa," he snapped.

"I don't expect you to be my everything," I assured him, unsuccessfully attempting to hold back the tears. "I just want you to be happy."

"I can't be the person you want me to be," he said with anger. "And, by the way, I'm still smoking. I've been smoking behind your back ever since you thought I stopped."

I felt like I had just hit a brick wall. *Could it be this terrible? He doesn't want to be with me? What else has he been lying to me about?*

"Do you hear what I'm saying, Lisa?" He interrupted my racing thoughts.

Anger brewed inside me, gradually becoming more powerful than the sadness, "I thought everything was okay with us. We were just talking about our wedding plans yesterday."

Luke let out a frustrated sigh. "Look, I'm not ready to get married. I don't really want to be engaged right now. We are moving too fast."

Luke pushed himself back on the bed when he saw my red face flaming with anger. "YOU ARE A COMPLETE JERK! I HATE YOU!" I cried.

"Hold on, Lisa. I'm not saying I want to break up; I just want to take it slower."

"You can take this ring and shove it!" I threw the ring at Luke, my blood boiling.

"Lisa, listen to me, I love you – I still love you," Luke stammered, surprised by the intensity of my angry outburst.

"I can't believe you made me think you wanted to get married, acting like you really enjoyed our life." I wiped my tears with a tissue and blew my nose, throwing the tissue on the floor.

"I'm just saying I don't want to be engaged. I want to stay with you, just as your boyfriend, not your fiancé."

Why me? Why does this keep happening to me? First Eddie, now Luke... Just when I think my life is moving in the right direction – then BAM – my life is over.

Luke reached up and placed his hand on my shoulder. I shoved his hand away.

I glared back at Luke. "Seems like you have everything figured out already."

When I saw how Luke turned his anger around, I realized he was telling the truth. He didn't want to break up completely. While I was furious about Luke breaking off our engagement, there was no way I would ever be the one to end our relationship. I needed him, desperately.

That Saturday afternoon I reluctantly agreed to going back to being boyfriend-girlfriend. My dream of getting married was no longer a reality. *Would it ever be a reality?* I wondered.

Over the next few weeks, Luke distanced himself from me, even though he said we were still boyfriend-girlfriend. I spent more time with Sally and mustered up the enthusiasm for my twenty-first birthday, which was just around the corner.

A month later, Luke and I went out to dinner. After dinner, Luke pulled into his parent's driveway. I reached for the door handle, assuming that we would go inside to continue our date when Luke put his hand on my leg to stop me. "Hold on, I want to talk about something."

I had a bad feeling. While I feared the worst, I hoped for the best. I put my hand on Luke's. "What's up?"

Luke looked down at our hands together on my leg. "I love you so much..."

"Love you, too – with all my heart." I leaned over to kiss Luke, but he put his hand on my shoulder to stop me.

My heart felt heavy. I peered up at Luke with anxious anticipation.

"You are turning twenty-one soon. You have your whole life ahead of you."

"Yeah – isn't it great? We are moving on to the next phase of our life together." I tried to stay positive, in hopes that my hunch was wrong.

"That's what I want to talk about – us and our life together."

Tears welled up in my eyes. The look on Luke's face confirmed that my hunch had been right after all.

"I think it would be better if you had a chance to be single. Be on your own. Have some fun."

Panic set in. *No, God. NO! This can't be happening. Not again.*

I glanced up at Luke, pleading with tear-filled eyes, "Please don't do this. What can I do to make you happy? I gave you space – wasn't it enough?"

"I'm sorry. The last thing I want to do is hurt you."

"Then don't do this to me. Please, I'm begging you! I need you!" Once the crying began, I couldn't stop.

"Oh sweetheart, I know you would do anything for me. You have already done so much for me. I just can't do this anymore."

I reached over and grabbed Luke's hand, meeting his eyes, looking for a glimmer of hope that he might change his mind. I saw nothing.

"You will be better off without me. I've given this a lot of thought."

"I can't believe you would do this to me. You know... know how much you mean to me. My... my... life... isn't complete without you in it," I muttered between sobs.

"I'm sorry, Lisa; it breaks my heart to see you this upset. But... it's over."

It was over. I knew it. The end. My unwelcome friends, misery and loneliness, were back.

Luke got out of his truck and walked over to my side, opening the door so I could get into my car and drive home.

It was difficult to move. I pushed myself up, stood next to the truck and looked up at Luke one last time, hoping for a miracle...

Luke wrapped his arms around me, then looked at me with his hazel eyes and kissed me – one last time.

If you are in a serious relationship, you need to have the courage to step back and look at it with complete honesty. Are you putting pressure on your partner to commit to the next step when he or she may not be ready for marriage? Are you accepting of your partner, or are you always trying to change him or her?

Someone with SAD is often less assertive and lacks independence when it comes to relationships. It's easy to understand that if a relationship helps ease symptoms of SAD, a sufferer may hold onto it with a death grip. And if a person is so full of fear, it's extremely difficult to gain independence.

As you can imagine, I was devastated after Luke and I broke up. I went right back to what I had done after Eddie. I searched desperately for a new man to fill the void. The issues I had on the relationship front added drama to my life, giving me plenty to talk about with Sally, Rachel, and my friends at work.

A few years after Luke and I broke up, I met Mike. Once again, our relationship moved quickly. He was as desperate to be in a relationship as I was. The immediate physical connection developed into some form of love. Mike came with a mountain of debt, child custody issues from his divorce, and, worse yet, alcohol issues. He drank even more than I did. A few short months after we started dating, we moved in together. I felt Mike needed me to help him get his life together. I would do anything for him and he knew that...

November 1993
Twenty-four years old
Dating Mike for nine months

I arrived home one night to find a home-cooked meal waiting for me. "Wow, what's this all about?" I smiled, pleased with a good ending to a miserable, anxiety-filled day. Embarrassing situations at work, the grocery store, and the doctor's office left me exhausted.

"Can't I make my girlfriend a nice dinner?" Mike asked.

I sensed by the look in his eyes that he was up to something, but I went along with it anyway. "Sure! I'm starving!"

Mike's bad luck hadn't changed; he had had a job for a while, but was laid off again. The custody battle continued to be an issue. He started drinking more – if that was possible – and our relationship had its share of challenges.

Mike flashed me his smile. "We are going to have a lot of snow this winter. It would be great to have a snowmobile. Don't you think so?"

I wasn't sure where this was going, considering Mike didn't have money to live on, let alone money for a snowmobile. "Yeah. So?"

"You know how much I love you – right? You know we will be together forever – don't you?" Mike looked at me with the love I craved so much.

I placed my hand on Mike's and smiled at him. "Love you too."

"Well...I was hoping you could take out a loan for me so I could buy a snowmobile."

I pulled my hand away, shocked by Mike's bold request. I had already loaned him money. I never imagined he would actually ask me to borrow money from a bank for him. If he didn't make the payments I would get the bad credit rap.

"I don't think so," I said.

Mike looked at me with big, dreamy eyes. "Please. Please. You want me to be happy, don't you?"

Would Mike leave me if I didn't loan him the money? Look at how long it took me to find him. I don't want to go back to being alone again. No, I can't go back to that – I need to keep Mike happy or he will leave me.

"Oh... All right. I guess I could check at the bank to see if I could get a loan."

Mike jumped up from his chair, wrapped his arms around me, and kissed me with a familiar passion.

When Sally heard that I had loaned Mike the money for the snowmobile, she was furious. She actually thought he was physically abusing me to get me to do what he wanted. From the outside, it may have appeared that way; however, there wasn't any physical abuse... it was just that I needed a boyfriend desperately and would do anything to keep him.

When I wouldn't listen to Sally's warnings, she went to my parents. My parents confronted me and I denied everything, even the part that was true, that Mike was taking advantage of me financially. My hands shook with anger as I left my parents' house. I was hurt that Sally had betrayed me. I immediately ended our long friendship and grew even closer to Mike.

Over time, however, something started to change inside me. I'm not sure if I was beginning to see that I deserved more respect, or if I finally heard what Sally had been telling me all those years, but the relationship with Mike ended in less than two years. Mike was the one to break it off. The difference with this break-up was that I actually felt relief rather than sadness. It made me wonder if I had been ignoring God's help, too, and if it might be better for me to stay single for a while.

Take Action!

If you are in a relationship, reflect on it,
open your eyes and ears and decide
if this relationship is right for you.

If you are staying in an unhealthy relationship simply because you need a boyfriend or girlfriend, or your friends or family have expressed concerns about your significant other, you may need to open your eyes and ears to the truth. You deserve to be treated with love and respect. Take some time to reflect on your current relationship and see if it's in your best interest to stay together or break up. Remember that a relationship, whether healthy or unhealthy, is not the answer to overcoming SAD.

Are you in a relationship with a boyfriend or girlfriend who is taking advantage of you? If yes, in what ways are you being taken advantage of?

_____

_____

_____

List three ways which you can say no when your boyfriend or girlfriend tries to take advantage of you again:

1. _____

2. _____

3. _____

What do your friends say about your boyfriend or girlfriend?

_____

_____

_____

A few months after Mike and I split up, Sally and I repaired our friendship. We were both very stubborn, but thanks to Eddie (who remained a friend in our group after our break-up), Sally called me and invited me to her wedding. Without Eddie, our friendship may never have been repaired.

The new attitude I had on the relationship front resulted in an interesting year of the single life. I continued to drink heavily and even started a second job as a bartender. I was able to drink when bartending, so I often did to calm my nerves. I met a new friend at work named Carrie; we bonded over happy hour sharing stories of drunken escapades. Although alcohol continued to help me socialize outside of work, it significantly delayed my healing. It clouded my judgment and caused me to take risks I would never have taken when sober. I'm surprised that I'm even here to share my story with you considering some of the dangerous decisions I made while drunk. As I began to heal, I realized that alcohol was only hurting me and that it would never work long-term as a coping mechanism for SAD. It only created more problems! I implore you to learn from my experiences. Alcohol is not the answer.

When I was desperately searching for a new boyfriend, all my energy went toward work or my search. I didn't spend any time looking inside myself, to figure out why I struggled socially. Then, I met Greg...

November 1995
Twenty-six years old

One night when I was bartending, I shook the dice cup and dropped it on the bar to continue a game of bar dice with a customer. I glanced over and smiled at Greg. He was a regular at the bar and we would talk on occasion. He slid his empty beer bottle forward to get me to come over by him.

I slid a fresh beer in front of him. "Here ya go!"

"So, I was wondering if you would like to go out sometime," Greg said while fidgeting with the label on his beer bottle.

I looked into his hazel eyes. There was something about Greg that intrigued me; maybe it was his little kid grin – always making me smile. Or maybe it was the way he would walk into the bar with his friends, throwing his arms up in the air and yelling "YIPPEE!"

So, I went out on a limb and gave him my number. I slid the napkin with my number over to him.

"Interested in dinner or maybe a movie?" he asked.

My year of independence as a single girl made me realize I deserved to be treated better, and since I thought guys would dump me anyway, I might as well take them for what I could.

With a few drinks in me by this point, I tipped my head to the side and gave Greg a flirty smile. "Both – dinner and a movie."

A few days later, I walked into the steakhouse where Greg and I agreed to meet for our first date. He wasn't there yet, so I grabbed a seat at the bar and ordered a drink. My stomach was doing flips. I wiped my sweaty hand on my jeans, grabbed my glass, and took a big swig.

I turned toward the entrance to see Greg walking in. Our eyes met. My heart raced. His broad, muscular shoulders filled his off-white sweater.

"Hey, sorry I'm a few minutes late."

"No problem."

Greg handed me a stuffed puppy with a single red rose tucked behind the ear.

"Wow! How cute! Thanks!" The smile I already had on my face grew bigger.

Over dinner, we chatted about our families, friends, and work. Greg was easy to talk to. Looking into his kind eyes calmed me.

Later that night, waiting for the movie *Seven* to start, we talked about the struggles we had both experienced in the dating world.

My leg brushed up against Greg's. Warm passionate heat rushed through me. I shoved a handful of popcorn into my mouth. I longed to kiss him, to have his muscular arms wrapped around me.

At the end of the night, Greg dropped me off at the steakhouse where I had left my truck. I fidgeted inside my purse, looking for my keys. Greg sat on the other side of the truck like a perfect gentleman.

"I had a great time!" I said while turning to look at him with desire in my eyes.

"Me too. We should do it again."

"Yeah, that would be fun."

I leaned over toward Greg; he met me in an embrace and we gave into the passion we had felt all night. We kissed. Our first kiss.

I drove home, wondering if I really deserved someone like Greg. Was he too good for me? Too normal? Was I really ready to be treated like I deserved to be treated?

The next day, Carrie and I chatted about the date. "I don't know, Carrie, he just seems like he might be too nice for me."

"You deserve to be treated nice."

"I'm just not used to being with someone who isn't all screwed up," I joked.

"Seriously, Lisa, just date him for a while and see how it goes."

For once, I decided to listen to my friend's advice. *Maybe Carrie is right*, I thought.

The relationship with Greg took off surprisingly well. The fact that I was more independent helped. Greg never would have stayed with me if I was as needy as I was with Eddie, Luke, and Mike. It wasn't easy to allow myself to be treated with respect, but it was easy to be independent because I had a life now. I worked full time, went to college, and followed an exercise program. My life was busy. This added balance; Greg and I were able to build a strong relationship while maintaining a sense of ourselves.

As you heal from SAD, you will realize that you deserve to be treated with love, kindness, and respect. You are a great person and have a lot of love to give. Don't let someone take advantage of you. It's better to be by yourself than in a bad relationship. The confidence you have in yourself will continue to increase and, if love hasn't already found you, you will find love.

What is your vision of a healthy relationship?

_____

_____

_____

List three reasons why you are worthy of being treated with respect and kindness in a relationship:

1. _____

2. _____

3. _____

Part Three

Fixing the Pain

Chapter Ten

Being Diagnosed

"A journey of a thousand miles begins with a single step."
- Lao-Tzu

From the outside, it may have appeared as if my life was in order. Greg and I were getting married, my career was moving along well, and I had some great friends, but on the inside, the disappointment in my ability to socialize without anxiety continued to grow. The Secret Pain controlled me and caused me to constantly doubt myself. I prayed to God for help. He was the only one I could be honest with about my emotional turmoil…

God, why can't You help me? Why do You allow me to live in so much fear? Why are my days full of misery? I don't want to live this way anymore. I don't know how to change. Now Greg and I are getting married and I'm worried about being the center of attention at my wedding. It's supposed to be the best day of my life; I don't want to be an anxious mess on my wedding day.

At thirty years old, I still had no answers, no rational reason for my social fears. I started wondering if this was just the way it was going to be for the rest of my life. I would always be afraid. What a terrible thought.

Then, something miraculous happened. One Saturday, I was sitting in my living room casually flipping through a magazine, when an article about something called social anxiety disorder caught my eye. I read about how people with social anxiety disorder have a fear of being watched and judged by others. The symptoms ranged from blushing, to sweating, to trembling hands (just to name a few). The article pointed out that people with social anxiety disorder experience a level of fear in normal social situations that other people experience in a truly fearful situation like being chased by a wild animal. I wondered if this was what was going on with me...

October 1999
Thirty years old

After reading the article, I highlighted the reference books listed on social anxiety disorder and ripped the page out of the magazine. Jumping up from the couch, I grabbed my coat and purse and drove straight to Barnes and Noble.

At the book store, I scanned the titles and found *The Hidden Face of Shyness* by Franklin Schneier, M.D., and Lawrence Welkowitz, Ph.D. I scanned the index for my biggest symptom – blushing. Five sections on blushing alone! I shook my head in disbelief as I flipped to the first section and read a story about a woman who blushed. She wore buttoned up collars year round to camouflage the problem. While standing in the book store with my mouth hanging wide open, I wanted to read the entire book right there.

Can this be an explanation for the misery I've experienced over the past thirty years? I can't believe there are other people who feel like me!

I slid the first book under my arm and scanned the shelves for the second book, *Beyond Shyness* by Jonathan Berent. Finding that book, I quickly scanned the pages. Information about therapies, changing negative thoughts to positive, using something called affirmations, and seeking the help of counselors jumped out at me.

Holding onto the books as if they were precious gold, I purchased them and immediately went home to begin reading.

I had struggled with social insecurities for so many years. All the prayers for help seemed to have gone unanswered. My social fears were ingrained into my heart and mind. Could this newfound knowledge be the missing link, and could putting a name to the problem and reading a couple books stop The Secret Pain once and for all?

The first thing I did after diagnosing myself was to consider telling my fiancé, Greg. Early in our relationship, we both shared that we had been shy in school, but I had never completely opened up about my current social fears. I realized the time had come. I needed to open up to him now…

As I lay in bed, I scooted closer to Greg, the coolness of the sheets reminding me that fall was upon us. My head was propped naturally on Greg's shoulder. We chatted about the day. I rested my hand on Greg's chest. The even rise and fall of his chest calmed me.

I hesitated about broaching the subject, but the calmness I felt cuddling next to him gave me the courage. "Um, I wanted to tell you... I read an article over the weekend that talked about something called social anxiety disorder."

"Yeah – so?"

"Well, from what I can tell, I'm pretty sure that's what's wrong with me."

"Oh yeah, there is something wrong with you all right." Greg laughed, trying to lighten up my serious mood. He reached over and tickled me in the ribs.

I squirmed away from his tickling hands and met his eyes. "I'm serious; I think I need to go to a counselor to find out if I'm right."

Greg didn't fully understand. He had overcome his own shyness by simply deciding that he didn't care about what other people thought of him.

"If I really do have this disorder, it also means I could actually get better."

Greg drew me into his arms and said, "Whatever you need to do, honey."

"So you aren't going to think I'm a nutcase if I go to a counselor, are you?" I joked, arching my brows and flashing a goofy smile.

"I already think of you as my little nutcase!" Greg laughed and proceeded to tickle me again. I laughed so hard tears ran down my cheeks. Tears of happiness are surely better than tears of sadness.

Even though Greg was a man of few words, I knew I had his support. I was ready to seek help, to get answers – finally.

Whether you believe you have SAD or have been formally diagnosed with SAD, it's important to know there is no magic solution to instantaneously take away all of your fears. You will find some valuable resources on the Internet, but proceed with caution. There are certain sites that will tout the "magic pill" that will take all your fears away, or sure-fire therapies that will solve your problems in 60 days – guaranteed or your money back!

Although the information wasn't as prolific when I started searching back in 1999, I did come across a few Internet sites where fellow sufferers commiserated about the disorder. They all shared stories about how miserable their lives were, and how they felt they would never get better. These sites only exacerbated my problem. I instantly fell into their pit of negativity. Doom and gloom – poor me! If you feel drawn to these sites before you start opening up to family and friends, just be

Healing from SAD is achievable!

cautious about the information you take in. The site www.socialanxietysupport.com is an example of a forum for those with SAD. Looking at this site recently, I noticed there are a couple of positive categories like "positive thinking" and "triumphs over social anxiety." When you visit the site, if you feel worse, then don't stay. Pay attention to how you feel. You know, deep down, if the site is the right one for you.

Look for credible sites, such as websites ending in .edu or .org. You can also rely on the websites of authors who published books on SAD. My own website is www.releasingsocialanxiety.com.

Healing from SAD is possible, but it takes time, effort, and determination. Depending on your age and the degree of severity, the healing process can take a few months to a few years. However, there will be successes all along the way, and in the first few months, you will experience some immediate relief. It's the deep healing, the long-lasting healing, that will take longer.

I have faith in you; I know you are determined and want to overcome SAD. I understand how you feel. I've been there. I have healed and so can you! You will see success; it's only a matter of time!

Chapter Eleven

Therapies

"If you believe, you will receive whatever
you ask for in prayer."
- Matthew 21:22

There are many therapies available to help you heal. Within those therapies, you will find different ways in which to identify and change negative thoughts. Everyone is different; a therapy that worked for me may not work for you and when it came to therapies, I tried a LOT of them. The anxiety I felt was so intense that I was determined to overcome it as quickly as possible. After all the years of pain and the prayers for help, I could finally take action and start to heal! I wanted to show God how much I appreciated His guidance by getting better. I wanted to see what the real, non-anxious me looked like. How would I act? Would people notice anything different about me when I wasn't afraid or embarrassed?

Early in my healing, I found out that negative thoughts were one of the primary reasons for my social fears. I had to learn to be the observer of my own thoughts. In other words, I had to observe myself having thoughts, and just like a scientist, examine those thoughts. I also had to explore the following questions:

❖ *What are my thoughts?*

❖ *Are they so automatic I can't hear them?*

❖ *Is my body simply reacting to the social situations out of habit?*

❖ *What am I worried about?*

❖ *What am I afraid of?*

❖ *Are my thoughts and fears rational or irrational?*

When I considered the answers to these questions, I realized I spent most of the day in my mind, from worrying, anticipating, or dreading my future to beating myself up about my past. The thoughts, when I was able to "hear" them, seemed like they could be irrational although I didn't understand why I allowed the thoughts to impact me so intensely. I felt like I was finally going to be moving in the right direction and dove head first into the therapies.

Take Action!
Take out a notebook and begin to explore the questions listed earlier on your own.

When you scan the list of therapies listed below, just pick one or two to try initially. As I said before, the process will take time. Certain therapies may be difficult to grasp early in your healing, so don't be discouraged; just come back to those therapies when your heart and mind are ready to understand them.

Type	Therapy	Timing; Frequency
ONE-ON-ONE	Behavioral Health Counselor	When you are ready; as needed
ONE-ON-ONE	Guidance Counselor Teacher Parent	A great option anytime; ongoing
INDEPENDENT	Self-Help books Audio Therapy Series	Early in healing; as needed
INDEPENDENT	Journaling	Ongoing; as often as possible
INDEPENDENT	Affirmations	Ongoing; daily
INDEPENDENT	Meditation	Ongoing; as often as possible
INDEPENDENT	Mindfulness	Start after some healing success; as often as possible
GROUP	Group Therapy	When you are ready; as needed

One-on-one Therapies

Behavioral Health Counselor

Seeing a behavioral health counselor may seem like a frightening step to take. Talking to a stranger about your deepest fears isn't easy at first, but once you start talking, it's usually difficult to stop. I speak from experience. Maybe you desperately want to see a counselor, but your family cannot afford to pay for one. There are always options. Investigate local or state assistance when it comes to counseling. Don't give up. If counseling doesn't become your preferred next step, consider the independent options I will cover later in this chapter.

In my case, because I was desperate for answers, seeking out a counselor was the first step I took. It was embarrassing to think that I needed to see a therapist. It was like admitting to the world that something was wrong with me. What if someone found out? In spite of my fears, I looked into the coverage for behavioral health counselors under my health insurance plan at work. I called to make an appointment for "anxiety" issues. Needless to say, I was excited and apprehensive about my first appointment...

October 1999
Thirty years old

I walked into the behavioral health facility on wobbly legs, clutching a notebook to my chest with damp hands. After checking in, I sat in the waiting room, all the while praying I wouldn't see anyone I knew. It would be devastating in a place like this, I thought; I felt the words "emotional failure" flash across my forehead. Of course, I was so caught up in my own fear of discovery that it didn't even occur to me that the other people in the waiting room were being treated for something, too!

I grabbed a magazine and tried to appear relaxed. I flipped through the pages with trembling hands. It seemed like forever before I heard a counselor call "Lisa."

I glanced up with fear-filled eyes, forcing a smile. "Hi," I mumbled.

I sat in a chair in the counselor's office. After explaining the therapy process, my new counselor, Sue, asked what had prompted me to set up an appointment.

I tried to breathe, but the air wouldn't exit or enter my lungs. My thoughts galloped like a racehorse, *I can't talk. I can't tell her what's going on. Oh my gosh, what is my problem? I'm such an idiot.*

Sue was waiting for me to say something. I could see the empathy in her eyes.

It felt like an eternity before I could form the words. "I always feel like people are looking at me. I'm sure people laugh at me and think I'm weird."

I expected Sue to say my concerns were ridiculous, but instead she said, "Tell me more."

"People, my friends or co-workers, must wonder why one minute I seem fine and the next minute I'm fidgeting and stumbling over words."

"I understand," Sue said, while glancing up from her notebook. "That must be so difficult."

Her heartfelt empathy helped me to continue. "I'm miserable and haven't been able to figure out what is going on. No matter how many self-help books I read, no matter how much I pray to God for help, there are never any answers. No solutions."

I continued to let out the years of pent up emotional baggage as Sue's pen flew across the page.

I'm not sure how long it was before Sue put her pen down and looked at me with an understanding smile. "Lisa, from what you're telling me, I believe you have what is called social anxiety disorder. It's treatable with therapy."

Did she just say treatable?

"And with time, I know you will be able to overcome this disorder."

For the first time in my life, I felt the light of hope shine upon me.

Finally an answer! I thought as my body filled with joyful warmth. I felt like I was a bird soaring above the water.

Free.

Hopeful.

I sat still and calm, but inside I was jumping for joy!

Sue shared details about the therapy techniques.

I soaked it up like a sponge. *Meditation. Journaling. Yes. Whatever it takes, I will do it. I will eliminate my social insecurities. If I do everything Sue suggests, I will be better in no time.*

I smiled at Sue. And so we began.

When I started seeing Sue, I didn't want anyone to know I was in therapy. Greg and my counselor were the only people I confided in about my deepest fears. Greg would listen to me, but I don't think he really understood the disorder. He would often tell me that I should just stop worrying about what other people thought of me. I knew Greg meant well and was trying to help, but if I had been capable of doing that, I would have done it ages ago!

As you can see from my story, having the counselor validate my self-diagnosis felt wonderful. To know that I wasn't crazy after all! To know that there was some hope for a better life! I want you to have a better life, too. And remember, for those of us with SAD, when we talk to our friends and family, they will love and support us, but those who've never suffered from SAD do not understand how difficult it is to stop worrying about what other people think. A counselor will understand the challenges with a disorder such as SAD.

Seeing a counselor isn't as scary as you think.

When you are ready to see a counselor, take the leap. It's not as scary as you may think. You are a wonderful, loving, and kind person. You deserve a great life!

Going into my second appointment with Sue, I still felt nervous, but this time I was also filled with pleasant anticipation about the opportunity to talk so openly with someone about my true feelings.

November 1999

Sue started the session. "How are you feeling? What have you done since we last talked?"

"I'm doing fifteen minutes of meditation in the morning. It's not easy to sit quietly, focusing on my breath for that long, but the CD you gave me is helping me to focus a little bit anyway."

"Yes, it's a new concept and it will take time. Your thoughts will try to take over when you are meditating; this is normal."

"That's for sure, my thoughts definitely wanted to take over."

"What else have you tried?"

"I bought a new journal and started writing down my feelings at least once a day."

"Are you noticing any positive changes?"

"Not yet," I confessed with despair. "The embarrassing situations are still happening and it feels like my symptoms are worse than ever."

"Lisa, you are making progress even though you may not see it yet," Sue assured me. In her gentle way, she added the words that touched my heart. "I believe in you, and remember God believes in you, too."

"I've been praying for so many years, but it never seemed like God was helping."

"He's there for you always."

"I hope so." I smiled. "I just wish I could feel better already – at least a little bit."

"You won't feel better overnight. The therapies you are going through will re-train your mind and convert the negative thoughts into positive ones."

"But how do I know what the negative thoughts are? How do I turn them around?"

"Well, first, when you start feeling anxious, focus on your thoughts. What are you thinking at that moment? Write it down if you can – right away – or shortly thereafter. Once you create a negative thought list, you can write the positive counter thought. The rational truth versus the irrational non-truth. Does that make sense?"

"Makes sense, but I am usually more focused on my feelings than my thoughts."

Sue nodded in recognition. "I understand, Lisa. I know it's difficult, but I want you to see that thought comes before the feeling. The thought triggers the emotion of fear, anxiety, or embarrassment, so it's important to recognize each and every thought you are having. Between now and the next time we meet, I'd like you create a list of your negative thoughts. Then next time we get together we will review them and come up with positive counter thoughts."

After that second session with Sue, I pulled together an extensive list of negative thoughts. It wasn't easy because the thoughts were so automatic, but as I added to my list, I began to see how negative thinking contributed to my anxiety. We met again and created the positive counter thoughts, which would serve as affirmations (which I will discuss in more detail in a future section). For now, here is a sample of negative thoughts and positive counter thoughts:

Negative thought	Positive thought
When I see someone I know at the store, I will be visibly embarrassed and she will think I'm strange.	It's nice to see people I know and I welcome opportunities to socialize.
People will think I'm very nervous and unsure of myself at work because I'm so high strung.	I am a confident, hard working employee who focuses whole-heartedly on her work. Others recognize these positive qualities in me.
When I'm visibly embarrassed in a social situation, people will talk about me behind my back and laugh at me.	In social situations, I will do my best. People may not notice my emotional reactions as much as I think they do.

In addition to counseling, there are prescription medications that can help to minimize anxiety symptoms while you heal. Initially, Sue prescribed a medication for me called Paxil but I didn't like the side effects and chose to tough it out and deal with the anxiety without medication. Sometimes I wonder if that may be one of the reasons why it took me longer to heal. I can't say for sure. However, I did pursue some natural supplements which did help to take the edge off my anxiety. With the professional advice of your doctor, you can decide whether supplements or medications will be a part of your treatment plan.

After I saw Sue for a period of time, she suggested that I see Dave, a relaxation therapist who used biofeedback equipment to test physical reactions such as brain waves, heart rate, and skin moisture. He would help me to see how much power my mind had over these physical reactions in my body. The first time I went into Dave's office and saw all the wires and electrodes, I was uncertain that this was the right step for me. But I was desperate to heal, and willing to try anything...

December 1999
Two months in counseling

As I sat in a chair prepared for my first biofeedback session, the relaxation therapist, Dave, connected electrodes to various places on my body and instructed me to think about an embarrassing situation.

"I want you to experience the full emotional reaction," Dave advised me.

"You want me to think of an embarrassing situation? That's easy!" I said.

Sitting there, I allowed an embarrassing situation to replay in my mind, *Walking down the hallway at work. Why do the hallways need to be so long? A person from my team is walking toward me. She's staring at me. I'm going to blush. Now she's REALLY staring at me and wondering what my problem is. Oh my gosh, what am I going to say? Maybe I'll just tell her it's hot in here...*

"Okay, Lisa, that's great," Dave said as he looked at the read-out on the monitor. "Your heart rate jumped, your brain waves took off, and the moisture increased on your hands, all just from thinking of an embarrassing situation!"

"Hmmm. I guess the feelings aren't all in my head."

"Well, they actually are in your head, but they cause a reaction in your body. It's amazing how quickly you can influence your physical stats with your mind alone."

Dave wanted me to understand how powerful the mind can be. My thoughts had spiked a strong reaction in my body, and I had only imagined an embarrassing situation in the safety of his office! Dave said he wondered how high my heart rate and moisture levels would be in a real-life situation.

"No wonder my emotions feel like they are always all over the place."

"Yes, this experiment really helps you to see the power of your own thoughts."

Biofeedback provided me with another level of understanding and another ray of hope.

It turns out that having an awareness of the mind-body connection was a step in the right direction for me after all, and it will be for you too. Once you realize how much your thoughts impact your physical reactions, you will understand the power of your mind.

Take Action!

Find out what options you have for seeing a behavioral health counselor.

List three negative thoughts and the positive counter thoughts.

Negative thoughts:

1. _____

2. _____

3. _____

Positive counter thoughts:

1. _____

2. _____

3. _____

How could a behavioral health counselor benefit you?

_____

_____

_____

Guidance Counselor, Teacher, Parent

Healing will happen more quickly when you begin to open up and start talking to someone. Is there a teacher, guidance counselor, parent, or friend you would feel comfortable talking to about your fears? Perhaps you worry about what other students would think if they saw you in the guidance counselor's office. First, it's none of their business. Second, for all the other students know, you are simply talking about colleges. It's no big deal.

When I was in high school, I was too afraid to open up to anyone. I chose to keep my fears buried, allowing The Secret Pain to grow like an undiagnosed cancer. My parents wanted me to open up and confide in them, but I was worried that I would disappoint them if I shared the fears I had buried so deeply. I thought if they knew something was wrong with me, they would take it personally. I thought they might tell me that my fears were irrational. I thought they would tell me to suck it up and just get over it already. I thought so many things and really had no way of knowing if my thoughts were actually true! This is why I never talked to my parents about social anxiety disorder until I was in my thirties.

You may think your parents are too busy to hear about your deepest fears, but give them a chance. Talk to them. Maybe their initial reaction is one of uncertainty. They may not know what to say or how to help you. You may need to give them some time to absorb what you have shared. Perhaps you find it difficult to talk to your parents about yourself. In that case, you could share this book with your parents and simply say that you have feelings similar to those explained in the book. They may want to do additional research to be sure they are giving you the best advice possible. If your parents are unable to help, ask them if you can see a behavioral health counselor (if you are ready to take that step). Asking for help is a key to your healing!

How might you begin a discussion with your mom or dad about your social fears?

_____

_____

_____

Independent Options

Self-help Books

There is a wealth of information available to you in the form of self-help. Books are a great way to become educated on social anxiety disorder. Just be careful not to overwhelm yourself with too many techniques and pay attention to how you feel when you read the information. If it doesn't feel right, put the book back on the shelf.

The stack of books I've accumulated over the past ten years is quite large. Typically, when I started reading a book, I knew in the first few chapters whether or not the book was right for me. Additionally, I found that some books were just too "over the top" at the time of my life when I tried reading them. This is where it's important to understand that some books will resonate more with you now, earlier in your healing, while others will impact you more later on in your healing process.

When reading self-help books, I highlighted sections that really hit home with me and wrote answers to the questions they posed in the book. Then, years down the road when I felt like I hadn't made any progress at all, I read through my old notes and realized how far I had come.

Capturing answers to the questions you read in books such as this and reviewing them later, as I did, could be beneficial to you, too. The review of your old notes will give you an opportunity to see how far you have progressed when you are having one of those days when you feel like you haven't made any progress. This exercise could pull you out of the old way of thinking which no longer serves you.

Here are some books that may help you on your journey:

❖ *Anxiety, Phobias and Panic: A Step-by-Step Program for Regaining Control of Your Life.* Reneau Z. Peurifoy, M.A., M.F.T.

❖ *Beyond Shyness: How to Conquer Social Anxieties.* Jonathan Berent, A.C.S.W.

❖ *Dying of Embarrassment: Help for Social Anxiety and Phobia.* Barbara G. Markway, Ph.D., Cheryl N. Carmin, Ph.D., C. Alec Pollard, Ph.D., Teresa Flynn, Ph.D.

❖ *The Hidden Face of Shyness: Understanding and Overcoming Social Anxiety.* Franklin Schneier, M.D., and Lawrence Welkowitz, Ph.D.

Audio Therapy Series

As you continue to find out about ways to overcome SAD, you will hear about cognitive-behavioral therapy. This is basically what every type of SAD therapy entails, but you may not always hear it referred to in this way. The cognitive-behavioral therapy helps you begin to change your thought patterns (cognitive) and, once you have made some success in that area, the therapy will teach you how to expose yourself to certain social situations for your learning (behavioral). The caution I have for you is to be sure you are starting to feel better in your head before you start diving into social situations – even those that cause little anxiety. Being too aggressive with your expectations will be a recipe for failure and disappointment. I had already been through one round of counseling when I felt I needed more. I decided to try an audio therapy series. Although I had felt some initial success after counseling, my social fears soon started growing again. The only difference was this time they felt worse. I felt as though I had failed myself, and that the work I had done to overcome SAD wasn't enough.

It's important to know that there are going to be setbacks. And the good news is that often times setbacks can lead to even deeper levels of healing. The Social Anxiety Institute offered an audio therapy series called *Overcoming Social Anxiety: Step by Step* and I believed it was exactly what I needed to get back on track.

A note from Dr. Thomas A. Richards
of the Social Anxiety Institute

"Behavioral therapy needs to be done in conjunction with the cognitive (i.e., learning) methods and the strategies that we know from research will work to change the brain. Gradually and gently move into safe situations, then move up the hierarchy. There is never any reason to take more than one step at a time. That's all you can do and it's all the brain is prepared to do if we want a PERMANENT change in the brain's neural pathways, which we do. So, one gentle step at a time with all of the methods and strategies in the 'real world' or in practical situations is the way to handle the behavioral aspects of healing."

A key learning from the audio series was a realization that I needed to be consistent with the therapy practices. There were many concepts I absorbed while listening to the audio series and I found that repetition was an integral part of the process. This made sense considering I had been repeating negative thoughts and behaviors for so many years. Consistency and repetition of new positive thoughts and behaviors needed to become the new norm. I prayed that I would be able to repave the roads in my mind with rational positive thoughts. I tried to be realistic and gentle with myself (although it was challenging at times), and gave myself encouragement and love along the way. With determination, I made it through the entire audio series and did experience many positive changes as a result.

The following are a few examples of concepts from the Social Anxiety Institute Audio Therapy Series that proved very valuable early in my recovery. I continue to use these techniques today, whenever I feel the need:

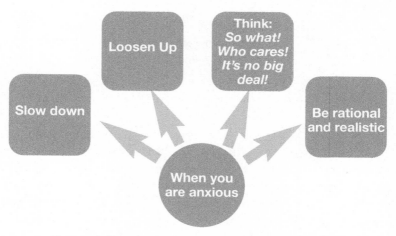

Image is based on notes taken while listening to
Social Anxiety Institute Audio Therapy Series

Slow Down

The "slow down" concept challenged the entire way I operated: walking, talking, and working fast. My Type A, high-anxiety personality made the "slowing down" technique difficult, but doable. The first area I targeted was learning to slow down my talking. When I was nervous I would talk a mile a minute. Talking more slowly didn't come easily. I would practice on my own at home before I was able to experiment in social situations. Walking more slowly was another area I worked on because I did have a tendency to walk quickly. When I was at work, and I felt my anxiety increasing, I would slow my pace. At times, if I was preparing to leave my desk for a meeting, rather than zooming off, I would pause and read the positive thoughts I had posted on my desk to re-frame my mind. Then I would take a deep breath and proceed to the next social interaction.

Take Action!

Practice slow talking by reading out loud
to yourself at home.

Loosen Up

The "loosen up" concept is about breathing deep into your stomach and allowing your body to relax like a ragdoll. It's learning to walk with limp arms rather than arms filled with tension. When I felt myself tensing up, I would tell myself, "Loosen up. Rag doll walking" and would gently shake my arms to remind myself to relax.

Take Action!

Practice the loosen up concept around
your home. Walk around with
floppy arms like a rag doll.

So What, Who Cares, It's No Big Deal

When I would think "So what! Who cares! It's no big deal!," it was typically related to something stupid I said or did, such as stumbling over my words, forgetting someone's name, or getting embarrassed when I saw someone I knew in the grocery store. When I left the painful situation, rather than allowing my mind to dive into a black hole of self-pity, I would tell myself, *So what if I was blushing! It's no big deal! No one said anything about it.* It was a good way for me to stop obsessing about the after-effects of an anxiety-filled situation.

 For more information on the Social Anxiety Institute's Audio Therapy Series, check out www.socialanxietyinstitute.org/audioseries.html

When you start evaluating treatment options such as an audio therapy series, you will know in your heart which approach is right for you. The amount of time you are willing to commit may vary, depending on how much anxiety you are dealing with on a daily basis. You will need to prioritize what is important to you, because you will need to spend time each day focusing on your therapy. The last thing you want is to increase your stress by adding a time-consuming treatment to your already full plate. Assess your obligations and, if possible, put some of your priorities on hold. What's more important? Getting all your work done? Or healing from SAD?

What types of social situations make you anxious?

_____

_____

_____

Of the different "when you are anxious" concepts (slow down, loosen up, etc.), which will you try first?

_____

If you were to go through an audio therapy series, how would you make time to dedicate toward therapy? What time of day would work best for you?

_____

_____

_____

Journaling

A journal is: "A record of experiences, ideas or reflections kept regularly for private use."
journal. 2011. In *Merriam-Webster.com*.
Retrieved December 18, 2011, from
http://www.merriam-webster.com/dictionary/journal

A great first step with any type of treatment is journaling. Even if the only step you have taken toward healing is reading this book, writing in a journal can help you in many ways. The most important thing to remember about journaling is that it's not about perfect writing. Don't write and imagine an English teacher looking over your shoulder. It's not about proper grammar or sentence structure; it's about getting your thoughts and feelings on paper. It's personal and you don't need to share your journal with anyone. Seeing your worst fears on paper can help you to sort through your feelings. You will find that, as you write, you will see words appearing before you that you didn't even realize were looming in your mind.

Keeping a journal is something I had done off and on for years. When I started therapy, it became an obvious requirement, especially since I wouldn't talk to anyone about The Secret Pain or the healing process once it had started. The journal was my outlet. The journal was my friend. Writing in my journal relaxed me and connected me to God. My journal entries became conversations with God. I told Him how much I loved Him, and I thanked Him for everything He had given me and for getting me on the path of healing.

When I was writing in my journal, sometimes it felt as though God was talking to me. Early in my therapy, I felt very discouraged because the healing was taking too long. It was as if God was talking to me through my pen...

> *Hi God, when will I get better? How long will it take?... It will take time. You need to be patient. You need to trust the process. Follow through on the therapies. The counselors are here to help you... I know I need to trust you, God, to handle these issues. It's so hard, though. Why does everything have to be such a challenge for me? My entire life. Why can't You make just one thing easy for me? Please.*

Farther along in my healing process, God reassured me that I was on the right path:

> *I am so proud of you, my child. You are love. You are peace. You are perfect just the way you are. I love you my child. All the answers you seek are right in front of you.*

The other great benefit of journaling for me was that it helped to ground me and pull me into a positive place. If I was having a lot of anxiety leading up to a social event, I would take out my journal and put my fears on paper. Then I would write positive thoughts, like *calm, peace,* and *relax.* Or, I would write about how great the social situation was going to turn out for me. Then, when the situation actually occurred, I felt better and less anxious. My frame of mind was so much more positive. It really worked!

Take Action!

Buy a new journal and
find your favorite pen.
Start writing today!!

Affirmations

An affirmation is: "A statement asserting the existence or the truth of something."
affirmation. 2011. In *Merriam-Webster.com*.
Retrieved December 18, 2011, from
http://www.merriam-webster.com/dictionary/affirmation

You are perfect just the way you are.
You are a loving and kind person.
You deserve peace.

These are true statements about you. I know them to be true and soon you will know them to be true, too. Statements like these are called positive affirmations. Affirmations are a foundational component to your healing.

As I mentioned earlier, issues with SAD come from the negative thoughts rolling through your mind on a regular basis. The key to changing these negative thoughts into positive thoughts is to use affirmations. Affirmations will retrain your mind. The affirmations are the positive counter thoughts to your negative thoughts. In order for affirmations to "sink in" to the pathways in your mind, it's important to say them out loud to yourself while looking in the mirror.

When I first started experimenting with affirmations, it felt weird talking to myself while looking at myself in the mirror. But over time, I got used to it. Since I had allowed the negative thoughts to stick around for so many years, I knew the change in my thought patterns wouldn't happen overnight. As I healed, I would change the affirmations. It all depended on what phase of my healing I was in at the time. Once I started feeling better, I sometimes took my healing for granted. I thought that since I was better, I no longer needed to take care of myself. This was always a mistake. Even when you start seeing positive changes in your life, stick with the therapies, especially affirmations!

As you become more aware of negative thoughts related to social situations, you will be able to identify positive affirmations. Your journal can be a great way to catch the negative thoughts as you write about an embarrassing situation. You may even find it helpful to have a way to jot down thoughts immediately following a stressful situation (e.g., in a small notebook or smartphone application). Write down what was going through your mind at the time.

To help you better understand how the negative and positive thoughts may compare, here are a few examples:

| I will blush and the person talking to me will think I'm weird. | • So what if I blush – will the person stop talking to me? No.
 • When someone talks to me, I will really listen and focus on them. |

| I need to do everything perfectly and cannot make mistakes. | • It's OK not to know all the answers.
 • It's OK not to be prepared for every communication that takes place.
 • It's OK to make mistakes. I am perfect just the way I am. |

| Why is everybody looking at me? | • People really listen to me when I talk and value my opinion.
 • People are kind and respect me. |

You may find it easier at first to take positive affirmations from a self-help book such as this, or you may prefer to come up with your own affirmations. Just don't be too hard on yourself. Remember that certain aspects of your personality are the true you. You may be more anxious than another person. That's okay. You are living the path you were destined to live, and the difficulties you face were meant to happen for some reason. It may never be clear to you what that reason is. Keep an open mind. You will begin to see your true self as you move through your healing journey. What does the non-anxious you look like? Have you felt real peace and calmness throughout your body? You will someday soon!

Take Action!

Write down one positive affirmation and read it at least once per day.

List some positive affirmations that could help you:

_____

_____

What qualities of your personality do you often want
to change, but upon reflection, realize they are
just part of who you are?

_____

_____

_____

What does the non-anxious you look like?

_____

_____

_____

Meditation and Visualization

To meditate is: "1. To engage in contemplation or reflection; 2. To engage in mental exercise for the purpose of reaching a heightened level of spiritual awareness."
meditate. 2011. In *Merriam-Webster.com*.
Retrieved December 18, 2011, from
http://www.merriam-webster.com/dictionary/meditate

Meditation will help you to calm down and listen to your inner voice. Through meditation, you can find out who you really are deep down. Often times the person you find is the person whom you have always been – the person everyone has seen – except you. Meditation can give you a sense of peace, even if it is only for a few seconds.

For me, meditation calmed my mind and cleared my thoughts. As I mentioned earlier in this chapter, meditation was something my first counselor suggested. She gave me a CD to listen to, but it wasn't as easy as I thought it would be. My mind would run a mile a minute, from worrying about work to planning the next day to reliving an embarrassing situation. It was, and still is, extremely challenging to stop the thoughts. But, meditation helped. Even though I didn't succeed at stopping the thoughts for the entire meditation, it still helped me to calm down and relax. Through regular practice, the amount of time I felt completely relaxed increased. I was able to take advantage of a technique called the relaxation response.

According to Herbert Benson, M.D., the relaxation response is available to everyone. "Each of us possesses a natural and innate protective mechanism against 'overstress,' which allows us to turn off harmful bodily effects, to counter the effects of the fight-or-flight response. This response against 'overstress' brings on bodily changes that decrease heart rate, lower metabolism, decrease rate of breathing, and bring the body back into what is probably a healthier balance" (Benson, 1975, p. 10).

To establish the relaxation response, I needed to touch my index finger and thumb together when I was in a deep state of relaxation. Holding my fingers together for a few seconds allowed that feeling of relaxation to become engrained in my mind. Then, when I was in a stressful social situation, I could touch those two fingers together and remember that deep state of relaxation. Triggering those feelings of relaxation would gradually overpower the anxiety.

Daily Meditation Exercise

This exercise will help you to focus your attention and calm your mind. You will need a timer for this five minute daily exercise. All of your attention will be directed to the process of breathing.

1. Sit down in a straight back chair with your feet flat on the floor, your spine straight and gently pressed against the back of the chair.

2. With your timer set for five minutes, your eyes closed, and your hands resting comfortably on your thighs, place all of your attention on the inflowing of the breath and the outflowing of the breath.

3. Whenever your attention wanders to other places, thoughts, or body aches, gently bring your attention back to the natural flow of breath.

This exercise can also help if you have a difficult time falling asleep, or if you are sitting in rush hour traffic, or just had an incident that you can't stop thinking about. Remove your attention from your thoughts and focus on your breathing.

Take Action!

Find five minutes to practice
meditation this week.

When you begin to practice meditation, you may find it helpful to incorporate visualization into the process. Visualization has many possible definitions, depending on where you look. The way I've come to understand it is that when you are doing a visualization exercise, you are envisioning yourself the way you truly want to be in a certain situation.

After seeing my first counselor for a few months, I decided it was time to experiment with the visualization therapy she suggested. I visualized myself confidently walking down the hallway at work, looking people in the eye and saying hello to everyone. I visualized myself sitting in a meeting, sharing my weekly updates while making eye contact briefly with everyone in the room. Just like Sue said, it felt like I was watching a movie of a confident me. I liked this movie!

The visualization can happen in the privacy of your home, when you are in a meditation session, when you are preparing to enter a stressful situation, or when you are simply having some downtime to reflect. The same holds true for meditation. Look at other alternatives to expand the opportunities you have to meditate. One of the buildings I used to work in had a relaxation room. I took advantage of that room and did meditation there on occasion. It was a great way to break-up a stressful, anxiety-filled day.

The visualization technique is a great option to add to your toolkit if it is of interest to you. The more options you have, the better, in my opinion. Just remember that even though you visualize yourself as confident and can see the way you want a social situation to play out, it may not happen exactly that way. This, too, takes time and practice. Don't be too hard on yourself. Just congratulate yourself on the fact that you did the visualization exercise. The more you practice, the easier it will become and the faster your visualizations will become your reality.

When you are ready to explore meditation or visualization, you can either listen to a guided meditation CD, a CD with relaxing music, or meditate in silence. The most important part of these exercises is taking the time to stop, slow down, and relax. You may find that your mind continues to run rampant about everything you need to do, everything you are worried about, and your inability to successfully meditate or visualize. It will come, over time; it's not easy, but you can do it!

What step will you take to begin with a meditation practice?

_____

_____

_____

What time of day would work best for you to practice meditation?

_____

_____

_____

Group Therapies

Taking in all these therapy options may seem overwhelming at first, especially when you see a section called Group Therapies. Group therapy for someone with SAD may seem like a fearful proposition. Contemplate, however, that the people in the group would feel much like you do in social situations. Add the fact that a counselor helps to direct the conversations and the result is sure to be a good one.

I was very afraid to participate in a group therapy session. Opening up to a group of strangers about my Secret Pain wasn't something I ever thought I would do, but my desperation for relief from the constant inner turmoil pushed me toward group therapy. By the time I considered it, I had already been through a few rounds of counseling and the audio therapy series from the Social Anxiety Institute. I prayed to God for help when I was feeling discouraged, as SAD symptoms took hold of me yet again. I wondered if group therapy could help me somehow. Was group therapy the next logical step in my healing?

April 2004
Thirty-five years old

Sitting in the waiting room at the behavioral health clinic, I peered up from a magazine. People around me were reading magazines. The tapping of a foot on the linoleum floor mixed with the occasional flip of a magazine page. I peered above my page and looked around to see who might be in the group with me. I even wondered if the counselor was watching us all on a hidden camera to see how uncomfortable we were before she greeted us for the session.

A few moments later, a counselor entered the waiting room, "Everyone here for the SAD group, follow me."

The bright fluorescent lights reflected off the white table and white walls in the meeting room. Everyone found a seat. I glanced around the room. Of the six group members, every one fidgeted with paper or a pen, avoided eye contact, or seemed extremely uncomfortable – understandably so!

The counselor asked us to introduce ourselves. I listened to the brief introductions. My thoughts would occasionally take over, *To be in the room with people who feel the same way as me feels great! They understand where I'm coming from. They don't think I'm crazy – because they know – they feel the same way.*

My turn arrived. "Hi, I'm Lisa and I've had social anxiety disorder for as long as I can remember. I've been in and out of therapy for quite a few years now."

The counselor reviewed the definition and symptoms of social anxiety disorder and discussed the outline from the therapy manual. "Over the next few weeks, we will start slowly, doing some therapy in safe situations – in your home for example. Then, as time goes on, you will be experimenting with social situations which you would normally avoid and report back to the group on your progress."

Sensing the discomfort of the group members, she continued, "Don't worry; I will give you all the tools you need to be successful in your social experiments."

The group therapy sessions continued week after week, soon reaching the social experiment phase. My first experiment was to go into a store and drop something – on purpose – looking around to see if people were staring at me.

As my husband Greg and I walked from our car toward The Home Depot, he broke the silence of my fear. "So, are you really worried about dropping something? What's the big deal?"

I sighed and wished Greg could somehow understand the pain I felt in social situations. "It's embarrassing. People will look at me and see I'm embarrassed," I tried to explain.

"But it doesn't matter what other people think of you. So what if they stare at you. Don't worry about it."

"Easier said than done," I sighed. "But someday I will be as relaxed as you, not caring about what others think. I bet you could go into the store with your hair sticking straight up and not even think twice about it."

"Darn right! How about if I mess up my hair right now before we walk in?" A mischievous smile crossed Greg's face as he proceeded to mess up his hair.

I stopped suddenly, signs of embarrassment covering my face. "NO! I won't walk with you in the store if you do that!"

Greg laughed while straightening his hair, bless his heart. He was only trying to lighten my mood.

We walked into The Home Depot as I attempted to push past my increasing anxiety about the experiment.

I can't do this. Drawing attention to myself on purpose! No way!

"Remember, honey, this is your homework. You need to do this." Greg wanted me to be happier and move beyond social anxiety disorder once and for all.

I breathed deep into my stomach and blew out all the air. "I know. I will do it. Just give me time."

Greg left me alone, upon my request. I walked around the store looking for the perfect item to "drop." Finally, I decided on a pack of sandpaper. Muffled voices and the squeak of cart wheels would occasionally catch my attention. I listened to my heart beating through my entire body. It felt as if someone had grabbed hold of my stomach and was gradually increasing his grip.

I picked up the sandpaper with a sweaty, trembling hand. I let the pack of sandpaper slip through my fingers and, SLAP!, fall to the ground. Reaching down to pick it up, I carefully peered around to see how many people were staring at me, and imagined that the entire store would be staring back at me. A few heads did turn and eyes were on me, but only for a second. Most people didn't look at all.

I DID IT! Nothing happened! People did look at me, but not for long. It wasn't as bad as I thought after all!

The behavioral experiments the counselor integrated into group therapy were very effective. This approach was something I had been introduced to before; however, now I had the ability to talk about the experience with others who felt a similar level of fear. The group members had varying types of experiments, depending on where they were at with their healing, but the goals and levels of support were aligned. The counselor had us set goals for areas we wanted to address. We then needed to write down behavioral situations that would help us achieve those goals. The behavioral situations were ranked based on anxiety levels, with low being minimal and high being a lot.

Low
- Speak up in a one-on-one discussion without hesitation
- Talk to someone new at work in the elevator or stairway

Medium
- Talk to someone new in a store
- Speak up in a group of five without hesitation

High
- Ask a question in a large group (150-200)
- Give a presentation in front of a large group (150-200)

The group members developed behavioral experiments to work through the anxiety producing situations they identified. The counselor helped everyone stay positive, occasionally interjecting advice. As I exposed myself to the behavioral situations I feared, I began to see more successes. The death grip SAD had over me was beginning to loosen yet again.

Exploring social experiments such as my sandpaper story could help you too. Just be sure to do these at the right time in your recovery with the right support in place. Whether you are meeting one-on-one with a counselor, participating in group therapy, or doing some independent therapies, discussing or reflecting on the experiences is an integral part of the experiment. Most importantly, the first step in recovery is to work on being more okay in your mind by addressing your thoughts. As I mentioned earlier, this is the cognitive portion of the therapy. The social experiments are behavioral and, when you are ready to experiment, start with social situations that cause a minimal amount of anxiety. Then, once you have some successes, move up the list slowly by choosing items with a gradually increasing amount of social anxiety.

Getting back to group therapy, if this is part of your journey, you will know when the time is right. Trust in yourself to know what is right for you. If you have an inclination that group therapy is your next step, but have some doubts, meditate on the questions you have. Pray to God for guidance and listen in the brief moments of quiet for His answer.

Be realistic with the expectations you set for yourself. You will be able to work through your fears. You will overcome SAD. You will have a more peaceful life!

In what ways do you think group therapy could help you?

_____

_____

_____

What is a not-too-scary social situation that you could experiment with?

_____

_____

Looking forward on your healing journey, what is the social situation you fear the most that you would like to set as your end state target?

_____

_____

_____

Getting Started with Therapies

As you can see, many therapy options are available to you. Every one is different and a therapy may work for one person, but not another. You know yourself, and once you start to listen to your true self, your non-anxious self, you will know what step to take first. When evaluating what you will do next with therapies, consider these points in the areas of communication, reflection, and respecting yourself:

Respect Yourself

- RELAX! Remember to breathe deep relaxing breaths into your stomach
- Cut back on sugar and caffeine which make anxiety symptoms worse

Reflect

- Identify negative thoughts and develop positive affirmations
- Read your positive affirmations daily
- Journal your innermost thoughts
- Give your anxious mind a break: Meditate

Communicate

- Talk to trusted family and friends
- Seek counseling

Chapter Twelve

Setbacks and Successes

"Peace I leave with you; my peace I give you. I do not give to you as the world gives. Do not let your hearts be troubled and do not be afraid."
- John 14:27

There is a reason why healing is referred to as a journey. The road is not straight; there are many curves that God places on your path. I completely understand this now, after my healing journey. It seemed like whenever something changed in my life, like a new job or moving to a new building at work, the anxiety levels in my body would rise back up. Of course, it's normal for someone to have anxiety when he or she starts a new job. But when I found myself in a situation like this, I almost always set unrealistic expectations. When I moved to a new building and needed to meet a lot of new people, I didn't realize that many people would define this as a stressful event. I was so wrapped up in my own mind that I didn't open my eyes to see that others had the same fears.

As I felt The Secret Pain gaining strength again, any success I had achieved was overpowered by feelings of sadness, anger, and fear. I prayed to God, asking Him why He would put me through this pain yet again, after I worked so hard to overcome it. The voices of my counselors rang in my mind: "Remember to keep up with affirmations and journaling. Just because you are better doesn't mean it's okay to stop therapy techniques." If only I would have listened, but no: I felt better and thought I could use the time I spent on therapy to do something else, like reading a romance novel or watching television. I would then wonder if that time had been worth it, considering the pain I was feeling once again!

When I felt The Secret Pain return, what I didn't realize at the time was that it meant I had achieved some success. How could I be experiencing a setback without success? Once I was able to see this, I would focus my mind on past successes, pull the positive affirmations back out of the drawer, start meditating again, writing in my journal, and reading. I would also look through my old journals and books I read in the past, which helped me to realize how far I had really come. Seeing the successes in print raised my spirits and helped me to stay positive as I pushed through.

Successes from my journals

At school the other night, I didn't get all flustered when the teacher called on me. I used positive affirmations and breathing to control my anxiety levels.

Last night I saw a co-worker at Menards. I felt my face getting red, but I still went up to him and said hi. Once I was talking to him, I started feeling calmer. It's interesting to see how I react when acting as if I am confident.

At work the other day, we had to go around the room to share updates on our work activities. I was initially anxious, but then I remembered my techniques – focusing externally and the peace zone. When it came to my time, I talked and did fine without having the typical adrenaline rush.

Early in my healing journey, I was determined to address SAD for many reasons. The first and most important reason was my wedding day. There was no way I wanted to be the blushing bride – literally – standing in front of a church full of people. One of the most crucial successes for me to envision and reflect upon was my wedding day.

April 2000
Thirty-one years old

After an engagement of fifteen months and nearly as many months of positive affirmations and visualization practice related to the wedding, the long-awaited wedding day had finally arrived. I smiled at my reflection in the mirror:

I am very photogenic.
Breathe.
I like getting my picture taken.

The familiar affirmations rolled off my tongue. On this day, I even believed they were true!

The sun filtered through the stained glass window of the church and rays of colorful light landed on my bouquet of white roses. The sequins and beads on my white flowing dress sparkled, and a pearl necklace accentuated my sun-kissed skin.

"Do you, Lisa, take Greg to be your lawfully wedded husband?"

Tears filled my eyes as the love I felt for Greg filled my heart. And even though I was standing in a church full of people, my heart and mind were at peace.

I looked at Greg, a knowing smirk on his clean-shaven face, his brown hair combed just so, his black tuxedo jacket defining his muscular shoulders. He giggled quietly at the tears I attempted to hold back.

"I do." I held Greg's hand in mine and gazed up at him.

"Do you, Greg, take Lisa to be your lawfully wedded wife?"

"I do."

"You may now kiss the bride."

Family and friends filled the church with applause.

We embraced and had our first kiss as husband and wife. Our love bonded forever.

The rest of the day was a blur of small talk, dancing, and eating. Greg and I stole a kiss when we could, knowing the happiest day of our lives would soon be coming to an end.

Lying in bed that night, my husband sleeping next to me, I prayed, *Thank you God for being extra supportive on my special day. The worries I had so many months ago didn't even cross my mind. It's as if the fear and anxiety had been completely erased and I had been given a taste of happiness, true anxiety-free happiness.*
Could it be true?
Am I better?
Finally – after all these years? All I know is, I couldn't have done it without Your love and guidance. Thank You for everything. Love you. Amen.

Have you seen some success since your own journey to overcome SAD first began? Is reading this book the first step you are taking to heal? No matter where you are in your healing process, I'm very proud of you. You are taking the necessary steps to make positive changes in your life. Trust that you are making progress. Stay focused on the positives in your life, even as you are pushing through difficulties and setbacks in your healing journey. Instead of dwelling on the negative, keep a positive mindset which will benefit you all around.

As I continued to deal with my own setbacks, I discovered that along with different phases of healing came new anxiety triggers, new and different situations that brought The Secret Pain to my attention. There were food triggers such as sugar and caffeine, which got my heart beating even more rapidly. There were work triggers related to the perfection and control I mentioned earlier. I would stop having caffeine, but then something would happen and I would feel angry that I couldn't have caffeine like everyone else, so I would guzzle down a Diet Pepsi. At work, when I felt anxious, I would dive deeper into the work I was doing, ask for more work, and then talk about how stressed I was to everyone around me. I would commiserate with my co-workers about how the company worked its employees to burnout. It's amazing how much worse these situations seemed when I talked about them to others. I didn't realize that the simple act of voicing the negativity aloud and having another person validate it, actually caused it to grow!

When it came to work triggers, I realized it was time to make some changes. Here are some quick fixes I implemented to reduce my stress:

❖   Just leave

❖   Say NO

❖   Delegate

❖   Take a step back and SLOW DOWN

❖   Make a list of what is important and stick with it

❖   The work will always be there – you will never be caught up

After that, I implemented a long-term change; I moved from a full-time work schedule to part-time. This wasn't an easy decision, but I knew my current state of unhappiness and stress-related health issues weren't going to go away on their own. The Secret Pain would keep haunting me unless I started to make some life-altering changes. I had to make a significant change for me and my family.

As you look at your life, you can begin to find the triggers that cause you more anxiety. Maybe there's a person who you feel more nervous around. Maybe you feel really agitated after having caffeine. Or maybe you have family drama that gets your heart racing. Listen to your body. Pay attention. All these heart-racing triggers in your life will impact you socially, as well.

*God will bless
you with
the courage
you need.*

Once you become aware of these triggers, then you can make some decisions about what you are going to do about them. Maybe it's as simple as eliminating caffeine. Maybe it's more difficult, like confronting a negative family member and asking him or her to stay more positive around you. The courage you need to take action and speak up will come. God will bless you with this courage.

Remember you will have setbacks – that's normal. Setbacks are an indication that you have achieved some success. Celebrate your successes along the way. Focus on the positives in your life. Setting your standards too high right from the start will slow your healing. Enjoy the small successes. Enjoy now! Be open to and appreciate the positives in your present moment. Positive thinking is very powerful. You can do anything you set your mind to!

What is one success you have seen as you started healing from SAD?

_____

_____

_____

What steps will you take when you are faced with a setback?

_____

_____

What triggers anxiety in you?

_____

_____

_____

Chapter Thirteen

Releasing the Pain

*"Sometimes God doesn't tell us His plan because
we wouldn't believe it anyway."*
- Carlton Pearson

The healing process for me has been an evolutionary experience. When I started therapy, I set my expectations really high and thought that "Voila!" I would be healed. Just like that! Once God helped me to discover what was wrong with me, why would He allow me to continue feeling The Secret Pain? Why would He allow it to come back? But now I've come to realize that every leg of my journey had a purpose.

The types of therapies I used over the years, the people I met, the level of healing I went through – everything, all of it, happened at the right time for me. The reason why SAD "came back" was because I never fully released it. I never stopped worrying about gaining everyone's approval for everything I did – the clothes I wore, the way I looked, what I said. I never stopped feeding into the negativity around me. I didn't truly love myself, even though I had worked so hard to heal and change my thoughts. My eyes started opening when I met a reflexologist named Laura. She helped me to start releasing the pain...

March 2008
Thirty-nine years old

I took in the décor in the familiar reflexologist's waiting room, a stone with the word "peace" on it, magazines and books about healthy eating and natural remedies. I scanned the reflexology chart on the wall, which showed how every component of our bodies is reflected through our feet. I picked up a reflexology flier, reading the benefits: "reduce anxiety and stress," "reduce headaches."

I reminisced about the events since my last visit. Reflexology was another step in my healing process. I reflected back on what brought me to Laura in the first place. The stress at work was too much; I nearly ended up having a nervous breakdown. At that point, any therapy I had done in the past was full of cobwebs – untouched – for at least three years.

Contrary to my belief that things would get better when I reduced my work schedule to three days per week, the anxiety worsened. Less time thinking about work and more time thinking about myself proved to be a recipe for disaster.

A friend recommended reflexology as a way to find out what might be causing my "health" issues. Even though I hadn't opened up to anyone besides Greg and my doctors about the fact that I had SAD, I had talked to friends about health issues like high blood pressure and general feelings of anxiety.

"Well, hello, Lisa! It's great to see you again!" Laura's smile made me smile. I felt at ease from the peace surrounding her.

Laura started the reflexology treatment and, as with previous treatments, she also started sharing insightful guidance and asking pertinent questions.

"Lisa, you have improved so much since last time you were here. What a change!"

"I tried really hard to follow your recommendations."

"You have the power to heal yourself."

I explained that therapy had been a big part of my life over the past few years as I worked to overcome social anxiety disorder. "Pulling out the therapies and reading Louise Hay's book *You Can Heal Your Life* made a huge difference," I added. "It was good to understand that my body *was* really telling me something – I wasn't just crazy or out of my mind – and I needed to find ways to reduce the anxiety I was feeling."

"Why do you think that God would put you through the pain of social anxiety disorder?" Laura asked.

Letting out a sigh and a laugh at the same time, I said, "I have absolutely no idea!"

"It may be so you can help others who are dealing with the same issue," Laura suggested. "Healing yourself gives you the ability to help others heal." Laura peered up at me over her glasses, her smile meeting my uncertainty.

"But how can I help people when the only person I have told about my struggles is my husband? My own mother doesn't even know!"

A knowing look came into Laura's eyes, "Your mom and everyone in your life will know, eventually."

I laughed again, thoughts filled with doubt rolling through my mind. *Sure, like I'm going to tell everyone about my battle with social anxiety disorder – now. After all these years. Like I need to have people watching me, wondering what a person with social anxiety does, how they act... Don't think so. No way.*

Over the next few weeks Laura's questions replayed in my mind. Per Laura's suggestion, I listened to Wayne Dyer's *Change Your Thoughts, Change Your Life* CDs and prayed for answers. I eventually realized that she was right. The only rational reason God would put me through this horrific pain was so I could help others. Why else would He have allowed me to go through so many grueling years of therapy as The Secret Pain continued to haunt me?

A month later, I arrived at Laura's for a reflexology appointment, "So Lisa, tell me what's been going on since we last talked."

Pent-up excitement burst out of me. "I've decided to open up about social anxiety disorder. I want to write a book to help others who are struggling."

"Wow! Lisa! That's wonderful news. I'm so excited for you! I have goose bumps!" Laura rubbed her arms and smiled.

"I have even started opening up about the disorder to my family, close friends, and a few people at work."

"How did that go?"

I shared one of the stories with Laura...

I grabbed the first few pages of my book, the book I had begun to write, and drove to my parents' house. As I pulled into the driveway, my stomach was a ball of nerves and my damp palms slid on the steering wheel.

It was time to tell Mom about my battle with social anxiety disorder, and worries kept bombarding me. Maybe she would be disappointed in me because I didn't tell her sooner. Maybe she would blame herself for my insecurities. Maybe she would look at me differently now that she knew something was wrong with me.

In my heart, I understood there was nothing to be ashamed of. Social anxiety disorder is a chemical imbalance that can happen to anyone. I realized that sharing the truth might help Mom and Dad understand more about what had happened in my childhood and why I struggled so much.

I took deep breaths feeling the air flow deep into my stomach.

Peace.

Breathe.

Calm.

The air flowed gently from my stomach up through my lungs and out my mouth.

I made small talk with Mom about the television show we were watching. A commercial came on and I knew it was time, but it felt as though my jaw was wired shut. It seemed like forever before I mustered up the courage to speak. "Mom, a few years ago I was diagnosed with social anxiety disorder."

Saying the words aloud to Mom caused all the painful memories to surface. Seeing a friend at the store and stumbling over my words. Having a co-worker comment about my "tan" face in the restroom at work. Wanting to speak up in a meeting, but feeling too uncomfortable to talk.

I shoved the painful memories aside and went on to describe the disorder. As I shared my feelings, the tension lessened a bit and my jaw loosened up. Mom's empathy showed through in her concern-filled eyes. "Is everything okay now?"

"Yes, I'm okay," I assured her. "The therapy has really helped."

She sighed with relief. "That's good, honey, but why didn't you ever say anything?"

"I was embarrassed."

"Oh sweetie, you know you can tell me anything."

"This disorder is why I had so many problems in school with being shy."

"Now I understand why you would always come home crying from school, run into your room, and slam the door. You wouldn't tell me what was going on back then."

We talked a while longer and I finally reached the point where it made sense to tell her about the book. "I especially wanted to tell you about it now, because I've decided to write a book about my battle with social anxiety disorder to help others." I peered up at Mom anxiously, awaiting a reaction.

Mom's eyes widened, "Oh, wow! That's great, Lisa."

"Here's the introduction I've started. I'll leave it here if you'd like to read it later," I said, laying it on the coffee table.

Later that night, after I had returned home, feeling good about our conversation, Mom called me.

"I read what you wrote, Lisa, and I wanted you to know that I think it's great what you are doing. You are going to help so many people."

Warmness flowed into my heart. "Thanks, Mom."

There was a moment of silence and then Mom said, "I thought I was reading about my own life."

"You did?" I gasped. "Wow, that's interesting."

"I understand how you feel, because I felt the same way when I was growing up."

Regret filled my heart. If only I would have talked to Mom sooner. I doubt my disorder would have worsened to such a degree if I would have had the courage to communicate earlier. Of course, I'll never really know…

Laura listened attentively to the story and then expressed her happiness about my ability to finally open up about SAD to my family.

"I wish I had opened up sooner, now that I know Mom went through the same issues. She could have helped me when I was struggling," I said sadly.

"Yes, very true," Laura said with sympathy. "But there's a reason for everything and I'm sure God has a plan. The most important question is, how do you feel now that you have opened up?"

"I feel wonderful!" I exclaimed. "I don't need to keep the pain a secret anymore. If I have a setback, I no longer need to keep it to myself; I can talk more openly about my feelings."

Laura had some additional questions about SAD so that she could further understand the impact the disorder has on people. I explained to her that in social situations, people with SAD experience intense anxiety and fear of embarassment.

Then she asked one of her thought-provoking questions, "Isn't it true that there is no such thing as fear? Why does the Bible tell us not to fear 365 times?"

Unsure of how to respond, I shrugged my shoulders.

Laura continued, "When you feel anxious, ask yourself what your heart is telling you. Listen to your heart, Lisa, not your mind."

I sat in silence, taking in Laura's gentle wisdom. "Laura," I said, "you have given me a lot to think about!"

Wrapping up the session, Laura leaned over and gave me a hug.

That night, I pulled out my journal, and questioned where my negative thoughts came from. What specific experiences caused them? Did SAD develop because of Tom and Martin teasing me all those years ago? I knew forgiveness was so important to healing and, at that moment, I forgave myself for allowing the pain to impact my life so significantly.

I love myself as I am.

I am on the road to recovery now and hope I can be healed from the anxiety and negative thoughts.

Amen.

I took a chance when I decided to try something new like reflexology and God was there. He brought Laura into my life. Thank you, God! Even after all the therapies, I still hadn't ever seen the real "me." I knew the "correct" way to heal and the "correct" therapies to use, but I was missing the key aspect of healing. The key was to be present, to love myself, and to accept myself. There was more to me than I realized. I couldn't see that those who loved me would be supportive and non-judgmental when I opened up about my social fears. This is why I stressed to you early on in this book that communication is so important. Trust those around you and open up.

Laura had suggested a variety of supplements; dietary changes, such as eliminating refined sugar and caffeine; and books and CDs. As with any therapy, I dived in head first with utmost determination. In one of the books I mentioned earlier, *You Can Heal Your Life* by Louise Hay, I found many new affirmations to add to my daily affirmation list.

My Affirmations from *You Can Heal Your Life*
I calm my thoughts and I am serene.
I realize all fears. I now trust the process of life. I know that life is for me.
I am on an endless journey through eternity, and there is plenty of time. I communicate with my heart. All is well.
I joyously release the past. I am at peace.

(Hay, 1999, p. 182, 207 and 215)

The affirmations I used continued to change as the therapies I followed changed. I even created a song with affirmations based on Louise's book. Even today, I continue to read affirmations every day and sing the affirmation song to myself in the shower. It's to the point where I pull the shower curtain back and the positive affirmations flow into my mind.

I hope that you will see the value in positive affirmations and that the use of them becomes a habit for you. Perhaps you will even think of other creative ways in which you can use positive affirmations, such as my singing in the shower example. The important thing is that you begin to believe in yourself, love yourself, and fill your mind with positive messages. And, as often as you can, listen to your heart. Surround yourself with positive people and things. You can accept yourself as you are – now – today – even if you want to improve and become a stronger, healthier version of you.

What are three qualities that you love about yourself?

1. _____

2. _____

3. _____

What is one alternate way you will use your positive affirmations beyond talking to yourself in the mirror?

_____

_____

What steps will you take to stay focused on self-improvement and positive learning even after you have healed from SAD?

_____

_____

_____

The healing journey continued and I took a new interest in mindfulness to further expand the meditation I was doing. According to the authors of *The Mindful Way Through Depression*, "Mindfulness is the awareness that emerges through paying attention on purpose, in the present moment, and non-judgmentally to things as they are" (Williams, Teasdale, Segal and Kabat-Zinn, 2007, p. 47). I've given you many therapies to try already, and this is yet another that you can explore eventually. The messages about mindfulness had been presented to me in earlier therapies (some of which I explained in the Therapies chapter); however, I didn't really "see" the mindfulness piece because at first I was focused on the bigger picture of the therapies themselves.

Mindfulness for me was about allowing anxious thoughts to appear, exploring them, and using my senses to become aware of my surroundings. What do I hear? What do I see? The idea that I needed to eliminate anxiety wasn't the correct approach; I needed to allow and just be. Focusing on my breathing would bring me to the present because my breath was present. How does my breath feel going down into my stomach and back up through my lungs out my nostrils? I could be at peace in the present moment because that was when I was at one with God. He gave me peace.

The concept of mindfulness may be difficult to understand at first and I can honestly tell you that it was confusing to me initially. When you begin, it could be as simple as watching birds fly through the air, watching the leaves on a tree blow in the wind, smelling the lilac trees in full bloom in spring, or simply sitting in your backyard with your eyes closed listening to the sounds of nature, paying attention to what you see, hear, and smell. Get out of your mind, feel life. Calm your anxious mind.

When you are ready, I suggest looking into mindfulness further. Don't take on too much right away; it's difficult to know what is truly working when you throw too many solutions at a problem, but keep mindfulness in your therapy toolkit and pull it out when you are ready. It could eventually be an effective addition to your self-improvement therapies.

As I moved into this phase of therapy, I gently explored my past. I know I was blessed with a loving family, encouraging friends, and supportive managers at the jobs I held over the years. Even though I was shy in school, my friends never judged me or criticized me. They loved me as I was – why else would they spend so much time with me? Of course, it took many years to realize this, but today I know the truth and have thanked Sally and Rachel for their friendship and loving support during my difficult school years.

All of the relationship issues I had over the years served a purpose, too. Eddie helped me to survive high school. Hiding behind him wasn't the best solution for me, but I didn't know any better at the time.

The trials and tribulations of my relationships with men were all a part of God's plan for me. Without all the heartache and rough roads to my independence, I would never have met Greg. He never would have stayed with the "dependent me" from the past. He fell in love with the "independent me."

The closeness I felt to God grew as I released my past, worked on finding my true self, and focused on the present moment. I was becoming more open to Him and His guidance, remaining hopeful and anticipating the opportunities He would present to me next.

August 2010
Forty years old

The sun sparkled on Green Lake, like diamonds floating on the water. The Christian writers' conference was coming to an end. The walk down to the water on the dirt trail felt very cleansing. I had to whisk spider webs out of the path. It was as if I was clearing the spider webs out of my mind, clearing out the emotional baggage. The experience of talking openly about social anxiety disorder to a group of Christian writers felt wonderful. God's love was all around Green Lake – I could feel it. I could see it in everyone's eyes.

The message God gave me at the conference was forgiveness. Forgiving myself. Forgiving those who hurt me. I have been down this road before, but as with all other therapies, it seemed like I needed to revisit it again – and this time I was truly ready to forgive. I was so thankful to everyone at the conference for welcoming me, for listening to me, and supporting me. I was embraced by God's love through these wonderful people.

After dinner, on the last night of the conference, it was time for the presentations. Earlier that day, instead of feeling anxious about reading my writing aloud, I experienced a lot of intense emotional healing. When it was time for me to read an excerpt from my book in front of sixty people, I was filled with nervous excitement. I walked up to the podium when my instructor, author Mary Pierce, introduced me.

I explained that I was going to read an excerpt about when I was first diagnosed with social anxiety disorder.

I started reading and looked up to make eye contact. I saw everyone looking back at me with so much compassion that it overwhelmed me. It took my breath away. One person was wiping her eyes with a tissue. At that point, the intensity of my emotions multiplied, so I clutched the podium and finished reading the excerpt without looking up from the page. It took everything within me to finish reading without breaking down crying, not from sadness or fear, but from happiness.

Applause filled the room. I returned to my seat and allowed some of the happy tears to surface. I had just read about my Secret Pain in front of sixty people! I felt like I finally reached the top of the mountain. My arms reached up to God in praise for His support.

The next morning, I drove through the windy, tree-lined road on the way out of the conference center grounds. Everyone's kindness, the closeness to God, and the peace I felt the entire week enveloped me. As I reached the stop sign before pulling onto the highway, I glanced up at the sky. I saw birds flying in a perfect circle above me. A circle of peace. Perhaps it was a sign from God that He was proud of me. Perhaps it was His way of telling me He was always there for me, to hold me up through difficult times, to allow me to be the true me, the real me. Finally, after all those years, I could see clearly. I could feel peace – true peace.

Thank you, God!

My Wish For You

As you walk down the path of healing, keep your eyes open.
Accept God's love. Accept His guidance.
When you look back, do so gently and with love.
Be easy on yourself. You are perfect.
You have always been perfect.
As you walk forward, when you fall, get back up,
brush off the dirt, and keep walking forward.
Trust yourself. You know, deep in your heart, that you are okay.
Keep your eyes open. See the beauty of your uniqueness.
See the beauty around you, in other people, in nature.
Accept God's love with open arms.
Feel the sun, rain, or snow showering you with love.
Feel God forgiving past mistakes.
Breathe. Feel the joy in the present through your breath.
Stay centered in the now.
You are okay. You are love.
You are wonderful. I send you my love.
I have faith in you and I know you will be okay.
Your determination and trust in yourself will get you through.

References

Anxiety Disorders Association of America. (n.d.). Social Anxiety Disorder and Alcohol Abuse. Retrieved February 2012 from http://www.adaa.org/understanding-anxiety/social-anxiety-disorder/social-anxiety-and-alcohol-abuse

Benson, Herbert (1975). *The Relaxation Response.* Copyright© by William Morrow and Company Inc. Reprinted courtesy of HarperCollins Publishers, New York, New York.

Bullying Statistics 2010. (2010). Copyright© Bullying Statistics, www.bullyingstatistics.org. Retrieved March 2012 from http://www.bullyingstatistics.org/content/bullycide.html

Changing Minds.org. (n.d.) *Type A and Type B.* Retrieved December 2011, from changingminds.org/explanations/preferences/typea_typeb.htm

Coverdale, David (1982). *Here I Go Again* [Performed by Whitesnake]. On Saints and Sinners [CD]. USA/Canada: Geffen/Warner Bros.

Hay, Louise L. (1999). *You Can Heal Your Life.* Carlsbad, California: Hay House, Inc.

Kabat-Zinn, Jon, Segal, Zindel, Teasdale, John, and Williams, Mark. (2007). *The Mindful Way Through Depression.* Copyright© New York: The Guilford Press. Reprinted with permission of the Guilford Press.

PACER Center. *Bullying Prevention and Awareness Facts.* Retrieved July 2012 from http://www.pacer.org/bullying/nbpm/spreadtheword/ key-messages.asp. Reprinted with permission from PACER Center, Minneapolis, MN, (952) 838-9000. www.pacer.org. All rights reserved.

Peurifoy, Reneau Z. (2005). *Anxiety, Phobias, and Panic.* (2nd edition). New York: Grand Central Publishing.

Richards, Thomas A. (n.d.) What is Social Anxiety Disorder. *The Social Anxiety Institute.* Retrieved February 2009, from http://www.socialanxietyinstitute.org/define.html

Weiner, Andrea. (n.d.) *Shyness: Protective Armor or Social Barrier?* Dr. Andie. Retrieved September 2012, from http://drandie.com/shyness.html

About the Author

Lisa struggled with shyness and social anxiety from kindergarten on. She was bullied because of her shyness and inability to speak up for herself.

She relied on various coping techniques to survive until she was finally diagnosed with social anxiety disorder (SAD) in her late twenties.

Together with her faith, family, friends, and a range of therapies, Lisa has moved beyond SAD.

Lisa is very open about the challenges she faced when dealing with SAD. She is sharing her story to raise awareness of the disorder and hopes others can feel the freedom and joy she is now experiencing.

Lisa grew up on a dairy farm in a small Midwestern-Wisconsin town of 3,000 people. She is the oldest of four children with two sisters and a brother. Lisa lives with her husband and son in Appleton, Wisconsin. She has spent the last 20+ years of her life in the corporate world in a variety of positions from secretarial to computer support to information technology consultation.

For more information, check out Lisa's web site at: www.releasingsocialanxiety.com.